Barbara Forisha-Kovach is an associate professor of psychology and Chairperson of the Department of Behavioral Sciences at the University of Michigan—Dearborn. She is also president of Human Systems Analysis, Inc., a consulting firm based in Ann Arbor that conducts management training workshops for corporations. She has written several books, including *Outsiders on the Inside* (Prentice-Hall, 1981).

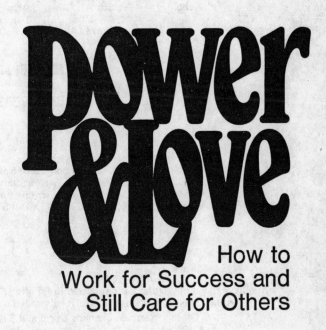

Power &Love

How to
Work for Success and
Still Care for Others

BARBARA FORISHA-KOVACH

Prentice-Hall, Inc., Englewood Cliffs, New Jersey   07632

Library of Congress Cataloging in Publication Data

Forisha-Kovach, Barbara.
Power & love.

A Spectrum Book.
Includes bibliographical references and index.
1. Love—Psychological aspects.   2. Control (Psy-
chology)   3. Success.   4. Interpersonal relations.
I. Title.   II. Title: Power and love.
BF575.L8F585   158   81-19253
AACR2

ISBN 0-13-687293-X

ISBN 0-13-687285-9 {PBK.}

1 2 3 4 5 6 7 8 9 10

Another version of Chapter Four appeared in *Building Family Strengths*,
edited by Nicholas Strinnett (University of Nebraska Press, 1980).
Other versions of Chapters Seven and Eight also appeared
in *Outsiders on the Inside: Women and Organizations*, edited
by Barbara Forisha and Barbara Goldman (Prentice-Hall, 1981).

Editorial/production supervision by Kimberly Mazur
Cover design by Jeannette Jacobs
Manufacturing buyer: Cathie Lenard

PRENTICE-HALL INTERNATIONAL, INC., *London*
PRENTICE-HALL OF AUSTRALIA PTY. LIMITED, *Sydney*
PRENTICE-HALL OF CANADA, LTD., *Toronto*
PRENTICE-HALL OF INDIA PRIVATE LIMITED, *New Delhi*
PRENTICE-HALL OF JAPAN, INC., *Tokyo*
PRENTICE-HALL OF SOUTHEAST ASIA PTE. LTD., *Singapore*
WHITEHALL BOOKS LIMITED, *Wellington, New Zealand*

CONTENTS

v

PREFACE

Writing this book has been a personal adventure for me, an exploration of my own views on power and love. I wrote this book at different times over the past three years while my own life was in transition. As my work on this book draws to a close, I am strongly aware of my own preference for movement over stability, for change over sameness—in fact, for being in *transition*.

I understand that not everyone chooses to live in this manner, but I also understand that in all lives there are times of transition in which the balance of power and love is recreated again. As I write, I hope that my own experience may help you see your own path more clearly so you may choose, wisely and well, your own directions—whether they be similar to or different from my own.

I am grateful to the many colleagues and friends who have helped me prepare this book by challenging my thinking, which enabled me to refine and further develop my own conceptual framework. Several who read the manuscript debated certain points and identified unclear passages, which helped to sharpen my thinking and writing. One of these is Barbara Goldman, whose work as coeditor of a previous book and whose editing on my current work have been invaluable. Others whose insights have been helpful in revision are my fellow consultant Glenn Morris, my research and program director Jeffrey Pilkington, and my secretary Mary Dubuc. I am also indebted to Marie Richmond-Abbot, whose painstaking and constructive review went to the heart of each chapter and led me to weed out the nonessential.

I owe a great deal to the staff of Prentice-Hall for their support and encouragement. The assistance provided by Lynne Lumsden, editor-in-chief of Spectrum Books, has been a continuing support for me in this undertaking. Lynne's warmth, openness, and insight have been one of the primary anchors in my writing career.

My deepest gratitude, however, goes to Randy Kovach: husband, friend, counselor, poet, editor, and life companion. His continuing conviction that *things will get done* has seen me through many roadblocks. His views on the human experience have added another dimension to my life that is reflected in much of the writing in this book.

There are many more individuals who have had a part in this work; those with whom my life is intertwined, including my children, my parents, my co-workers, and my students. Although these individuals have helped to shape this book, the final product is my responsibility. Whatever errors of thought or vision appear throughout this volume are mine alone. However, much that is good has arisen from the support and encouragement of family, friends, and colleagues.

Barbara Forisha-Kovach

INTRODUCTION

Psychologists have generally agreed that a high level of personal development involves both power and love, the capacity to work creatively and to care for others. Traditionally, however, power and love have been separated from each other; the powerful functions have been assigned to men and the loving ones to women. (Some have argued that women and men are both powerful and loving, though each sex historically may have demonstrated too little of one or both qualities.) Furthermore our Western culture has held power in higher esteem than love, so that the private has yielded to the public sphere, and woman has bowed to man.

Both men and women have begun to recognize the disadvantages of separating these two basic dimensions of human existence: we have been creating separate species and partial human beings. Today, however, women and men are both struggling to regain their disowned selves as women reach for power and men explore their feelings for self and others. Although we are in the process of change, the cultural beliefs are so deeply ingrained in us all that women have difficulty separating power from their concern with interpersonal relations and men have trouble reaching out to others without confusing the desire to care with the wish to maintain control. Both sexes, in different ways, have difficulty disentangling power and love.

Power is the capacity to "get something done." We all require power in order to survive and to act. The root of the word *power*, in Latin, means *I can.* Yet the term power has sometimes been viewed negatively, primarily as domination or manipulation of others. For this reason most individuals, particularly women, say they do not want power, even as they are striving for more of it.

Love, on the other hand, is the full acceptance of other human beings in all their uniqueness and individuality. Whereas power separates us from others, love brings us together with one another on a plane where all human beings are equal. Power, an essential component of human life, leads to aloneness, separateness, and distance. Love, the other necessary component of human life, is the experience of relatedness, mutuality, and communion. For high levels of human development, individuals must integrate power and love, which are not antagonists but companions. Power alternating with love assures us of both our individuality and our relatedness.

In our society, men are groomed for the realm of power and women are trained for a world of love. Men thus find themselves pinioned to a world view in which power becomes all, in which "greater than" and "less than" are the only viable categories, and in which they experience their separateness from others—and the accompanying despair. Men find, generally, that they are unable to leave power behind when they enter interpersonal relationships and the intrusion of the issue of control into areas where it does not belong often sets awry personal relationships. Men have learned, in the school of power, that they are either in control or they are not, and thus they allow the issue of control to distort the promise of love, since genuine love tolerates only equality and wilts under the impact of an imposed power structure.

Women, on the other hand, subvert love by believing that the mythology of human equality is appropriate in all situations. While women "get things done" they are concerned that no one feels hurt or inconvenienced, and that everyone feel comfortable and, above all, equal. In fact, this is a distortion of another kind. In the world of "getting things done," we are not all equal and in any given situation, one person will have more highly developed skills than another. Thus women allow the mythology of equality, the myth of love, to intrude in areas in which it does not belong. As a result they often have difficulty in acknowledging their talents or in directing the accomplishment of a task. Often women get things done by pleasing, placating, and serving others, and calling this love. This, in fact, is not love but manipulation. Like second-class citizens everywhere, women have learned how to wield power to meet their own needs. Thus when men emphasize power over love, they are perverting power into domination; when women emphasize love other power, they are likely to use love for manipulation.[1]

Full human development, however—to the extent that such ever occurs on this earth—encompasses both love and power. In the integration of power and love, both forces emerge in their highest forms.

In this book, the expression of love and power in human lives is examined in a variety of settings, in the best of times and the worst of times, and in the lives of children, adolescents, and adults. The conflicts of power and love are examined in relationships between women and men, in their

---

[1] I am indebted to Rollo May's *Love and Will* (New York: W.W. Norton & Co., Inc., 1969) for my first contact with this concept of love and power.

personal lives and in the workplace. Finally, the question is asked (but not necessarily answered), what lies beyond power and love, or, are these two dimensions the sum total of our existence?

Throughout the various explorations of power and love, the theme of change, of transition, is constant. This is a book about change. The separation of power and love is not as distinct as it was in previous generations. Women are beginning to accept power as a part of their lives, just as men are learning to accept love as an important factor in theirs. Writing this book has clarified my own thinking, both about where I have been and where I now am. I hope that it may also reflect the experience of others, provoke argument and discussion, and thus be part of the clarification process that we all undergo in times of transition.

PART I

DEVELOPMENTAL PATHWAYS

CHAPTER ONE

GROWING UP AND GROWING DOWN: THE PROBLEM WITH CHILDREN

What images do we have of a child's world? On television, in magazines, and in the aisles of every department store, children are portrayed as sweet and smiling creatures, the well-dressed owners of bright, shiny toys, and the doted-upon objects of fond parents. Small girls play with dolls, and now sometimes with trucks; their hair is curled and braided. Little boys play with trucks, rarely with dolls; they wear miniature blue jeans and football T-shirts. Parents smile benevolently in the background. Childhood, the image suggests, is a carefree adventure in the world of love.

Yet, having watched my own children pass through these years, I am assailed by another image. Childhood can also be visualized as a jungle gym, where each child jostles for position at the top. In this image, hair is not always combed, clothes and toys are as often muddied and broken as pressed and shiny, and parents are not always benevolent. In early childhood both boys and girls reach for the top. Later, the boys emerge as victors while the girls cheer them on; the boy who claims victory at the top is encouraged by a number of girls at the bottom. This image suggests a world not of love but of power, a world of winners and losers, victors and vanquished.

Which image carries more weight in the lives of children during their early school years, between the ages of five and twelve? Are these years more accurately visualized as a warm exploration of the circle of love or as a struggle for achievement on the ladder of power? My own experience has convinced me that during these years children become well-acquainted with the realities of power. They are scared of things that are stronger than they are. They populate their night world with overwhelming animals who chase them in the dark. They dream of being strong themselves and chasing others in the dark. The world of the young is divided into big and little, strong and weak.

If power were all our children knew, however, would they explore their world as fearlessly as they do? If their existence were solely dependent on the exercise of power, it seems likely that they would be more devious, more clever, and even more insistent in their demands. Rather, for most children, there is a fallback position. In infancy, they knew a world in which they were nurtured and cared for, in which older people—sometimes terrifying but often comforting—met their needs. They learned instinctively to trust that, after all, things would turn out all right. It is against this background that they can enter the world of their peers and of outside authority to find their measure in terms of power more than love.

CHILDREN AND THEIR PEERS: BEING BEST

For several years, I collected the writings of my daughter, Deborah. Prodded by the requirements of graduate school courses in child development, I also recorded episodes in her life which struck me as particularly significant. This collection of notes, both hers and mine, covers her years from five until nine. These writings illuminate the emphasis on power which apparently is common to most children. Among the notes I wrote in Debbie's sixth year were the following:

Four children were playing on the patio of our apartment. Tina and Debbie stood on an orange rectangular footstool. Tina said, "Let's play Wizard of Oz. I am the good witch." "I'm the bad witch," said Debbie. "Who will be Dorothy?" "I won't be Dorothy," said Gigi. "I won't either," echoed David. The children's voices rose as they argued with each other.

"I know," said Tina, "let's play Jesus Christ." "That's a good idea," Debbie agreed. "This is the Jesus Christ stand," proclaimed Tina, climbing back on the orange stool. "Yes," said Debbie, climbing up beside Tina, "but it's also the God Almighty stand." "You can be God, too," Debbie consoled David. "I don't want to play," said Gigi.

Five minutes later, Tina was about twenty-five yards away in the middle of the communal yard, surrounded by hundreds of windows in the apartment complex. She had relinquished her orange footstool for a stepladder. She was waving a stick over a cat, muttering incantations and lifting its spirit heavenward. Debbie, from her perch on the orange stool, waving another stick, commanded her friend at the top of her voice, "Jesus Christ! Come here!" With matching volume, Tina called back, "God Almighty! I'm busy!"

Tina and Debbie were playing tug-of-war with a gameboard, each demanding that she be first to play. They were glaring at each other with fierce determination. As I entered the room, they continued to pull on the gameboard, but turned their heads and shouted at me in unison, "I want to be first!" As they saw I was going to be reasonable about this (reason being out of the question), they united together, arms around each other's shoulders. One pair of blue eyes and one pair of brown eyes looked up at me, as the girls stated clearly and as one, "We always want to be first!"

As the year progressed, each girl learned to be more subtle in her desire to be first. Once, playing Snow White, Deborah sweetly suggested that Tina would be a perfect princess, and that she ought to take the lead role. It was several minutes before Tina realized that her chief contribution to their play was to sleep throughout the entire script while Deborah executed heroic deeds which would save her from her plight. At that point, Tina—who had been bemused by the idea of being a perfect princess—awoke abruptly from her sleep, stamped her foot, said, "This isn't fair!", and promptly rearranged the script and cast of characters.

Deborah and her friends played imaginary games of power in which they competed to be first. Sometimes the struggle was more real when their group confronted other groups from a nearby area. It seemed to an objective observer that the group which could make the most noise and shout the greatest threats to life and limb at the other party won the field. In both the games and the confrontations, there was little physical conflict or lasting animosity. These children were testing the world and learning the rules of the game. They were capable of learning many different sets of rules, as is clear in the next anecdote, also from my notes of that year.

Debbie is five years old and tolerates school with absolutely no enthusiasm. In November I am called in for teacher conferences about her recalcitrance. As the teacher glares at me with piercing eyes and pinches my arm, I find myself firmly on the side of my daughter. Talking with the principal later and unable to remove Debbie from the class (the teacher was later removed for incompetence), I decide to also tolerate, without enthusiasm, Deborah's first year of school.

In March, I shudder at opening another report card, and am startled when it reads, "Debbie is a lovely girl and a pleasure to have in class." In astonishment I ask my daughter, "Why does your teacher think you're doing so well all of a sudden?"

"Oh, that's easy. I'm the best in the class," she reponds nonchalantly.

"What do you have to do to be best?" I ask suspiciously.

"I keep my mouth shut and stand in line," says Debbie, as if anyone could see what ought to be obvious.

There are lots of ways to be "best," from playing God Almighty to keeping one's mouth shut and standing in line. Our children learn the various means to power: they learn to pretend and to dream, to unite with others, and to give in when their force is less than that opposing them. Sometimes they have a bad year (or years) in which the balance of winning and losing is set askew, and they learn the resignation and resentment of continual defeat. Yet for most children this is but a temporary experience.

Between eight and nine years of age, my daughter went through such a period. Having moved to a new environment, she did not learn quickly the new rules of the game and she often found the balance of power on the other side. Grateful for one or two friends, she was beleaguered by most of her peers. In bits of writing scattered under her bed, I found her airing her dissatisfaction with her classmates.

Peggy is really mean. She always chases me after school and at recess. She also says things like that I love Brad but I don't. I hate him.

I like Rita a little bit but usually I hate her. Once when I saw everyone throwing their coats up on the fence (and they stuck because the wind was blowing so hard) I came up and threw mine too and Rita was up on the fence and she put it up on the very top. I got it down at last when the wind stopped blowing so.

Karen is very dum. Who does she think she is bossing everyone around? She always says things like, "God, you don't ever zip your coat up!" Who cares if I don't zip my coat up?

Black and white, nice and mean, love and hate, the categories of the child's world are very clear. Categories so clearly defined are part of the world of power, where distinctions are carefully made, and no one is the equal of another. Love in this context has little to do with compassion or warmth. Rather, it is a measure of association. If one is careful, one strives to love (like) the powerful and careful to hate (avoid, dislike) the powerless. Deborah, often powerless and therefore disliked, would not abide taunted associations with others among the powerless (for example, Brad), but strove, in her better moments, only to be aloof from the battle.

CHILDREN AND THEIR PARENTS: THE POWER OF AUTHORITY

Dissatisfaction with peers is only part of the picture. Children also confront power at home. "Bigger" is always "stronger", at least in a child's eyes; parents are, therefore, always stronger and more powerful. When one is on good terms with power, one can identify with the parents and bask in their strength. When one is not on good terms with power, the parent becomes, at least occasionally, the enemy. Hence, some of Deborah's animosity was directed at us. Sometimes I used her ability to write and verbalize to deflect this animosity. One of her writings below was obviously required, the other spontaneous.

I get angry when . . .

1. Mommy sends me to my room to do stupid stuff like this.
2. Somebody hurts me.
3. My brother keeps on doing dum things.

What I can do about it is . . .

1. Control it
2. LAUGH
3. GIGGLE
4. SCREAM!!!

Dear Parents,

I am running away from home. I may be back when I feel better. I think my ideas are very good and if you don't think so you are very dum.

Your unloving daughter

Even so, the resentment of this period, for Deborah, was lightened by moments of flight, frolic, and compassion, in which a recognition of a shared plight of human beings makes its appearance. In her dreams of this period, which she wrote down, she is often chased by bears who pop out at her in grocery stores, on bike rides, and in forest scenes. But among these dreams are two others.

It was Sunday. I was playing at the park. Suddenly, a whole bunch of boys started chasing me. I jumped up and ran away. I was running so fast that I started to fly! It was really cool (and cold). I looked down at the boys below who were staring up at me and I wasn't watching where I was flying and I almost bumped into a bird!

It was Saturday. Me and my brother were eating ice cream. Suddenly he fell asleep and his head landed in the ice cream! I thought it was a little funny. But instead of laughing I woke him up and washed his face for him.

For Deborah, I think, this was a time when power loomed large and love was generally used as a weapon in the contest of strength. But power, though predominant, was not the last word in her situation. Occasionally, glimpses of compassion showed through. To what extent does my daughter's experience reflect the condition of growing up female in our society as opposed to male? And, if we can conclude that this experience can be generalized what then do we want to do about it? Can we do anything about it? These are the questions which will be addressed in the remainder of this chapter as we examine the requirements of the world we live in, the course of individual development, and the impact of our own perceptions upon the young.

THEORY: ERIKSON AND PIAGET

In search of answers to these questions, we turn first to two prominent theorists in child development, Erik Erikson and Jean Piaget, each a giant in his field. Erikson has focused on emotional development and Piaget on cognitive or intellectual development.

LEARNING BY DOING

According to Erikson, childhood is the stage of "industry" in which children learn how to do the things required by their culture.[1] During this time, children develop a sense of competence, of being able to cope with the world, or—alternately—they develop a sense of inferiority. In school, they

---

[1] Erik Erikson's theory is explained in many of his own books and articles as well as in those by others. The first conceptualization was published in *Childhood and Society* (New York: W.W. Norton & Co., Inc., 1950) and expanded upon in *Identity: Youth and Crisis* (New York: W.W. Norton & Co., Inc., 1968).

learn the rules of their culture, the boundaries for their world. On the playground, they learn how to test their skills with peers. At home they learn how to help out, clean their rooms, take care of their possessions, and behave toward guests. In all arenas, the babyhood is over, the stage when "anything goes", when misbehavior is adorable and cute. Rather, in middle childhood, young people are old enough to learn not only the rules of spelling and arithmetic, but the codes of proper behavior. This is a stage of learning how to *do*, and doing is associated with power, not love.

Erikson's emphasis on doing is compatible with Piaget's emphasis on rule-following. For Piaget, this is the age of *concrete thinking*, in which children learn the rules and the categories handed to them by the external world, and they follow those rules.[2] There is a black and a white, a right and a wrong, for most issues. There are definitions which say this is mine and this is yours. Furthermore, they learn that there are some who are more powerful than others. These are the authorities and the rule-makers. If these larger-than-life people have said it is so, then it must be so. At this age, authority is obeyed, feared, and sometimes admired.

Piaget particularly emphasizes the inability of children of this age to see beyond themselves. As they learn the categories of the world, they still do not have the capacity to understand themselves; hence, they cannot understand others. The ability to understand the position of another, to stand in someone else's shoes, is part of learning how to love. Children of this age are still too bound by their own perspective to really grasp what another might be thinking and feeling; they are not yet ready to love.

This is only one stage of childhood; children experi-

[2] Jean Piaget's theory is given in brief in *Psychology and the Child*, coauthored by Barbel Inhelder (New York: Basic Books, 1968), but is perhaps more easily read in *The Developmental Psychology of Jean Piaget*, by J. H. Flavell (New York: D. Van Nostrand, 1963).

ence many times the worlds of power and love before they are ready, as mature adults, to experience the full impact of either. In infancy, they received their first knowledge of love, as they were cared for and nurtured by others. As babies and then toddlers, they came to trust (or not to trust) those about them and the world in general, according to the degree to which they experienced themselves as loved by others. Infants also experienced power when nurturing was refused and when self-will was challenged. Yet, the primary experience of infancy is most likely one of love.

GOING BEYOND THE FAMILY

Secure in this background, children then pass into childhood. Still embedded in their families, certain of their origins and their place in the world, they explore the external world and venture into the world of power. They have much to see and to learn: There are schools, teachers, neighborhoods, and friends with which to reckon. Everything fits into its appropriate slot: black and white, right and wrong. There are few gray areas for children of this age.

In a world where there is a right and a wrong, it is better to be right than wrong. Intent on learning the "rights" of the world as quickly as possible, children are rule-bound and realistic. They are learners, climbers. There is only "mine" and "yours" and very rarely "ours."

By the end of childhood they have had their initial exposure to love and power. They still know love as receiving, not giving, and power as a measurement of strength, rather than the capacity to act. They are still apprentices to the system, struggling to be on the right side of the line wherever the line is drawn. They hedge their bets by avoiding all activities, people, and things which might fall on the wrong side. Other children who are thus suspect are not extended a helping hand. Instead their peers will hold their noses and hiss "Poison" at the potentially objectionable parties. Children of this age would rather be safe than sorry. Yet, it is possible that they grow from this place to another, learning more about both love and power as they grow into mature adults.

GIRLS AND BOYS: THE EMERGING DIFFERENCES

If the world of children is a world of power, Deborah's world is perhaps not uncharacteristic of that of her peers. Yet she is a girl, and her experience is necessarily a female, as well as a human, experience. Can we generalize her experience to all children or only to 51 percent of that population? In other words, we might ask, how different are boys and girls at this age? When do the boys come to stand at the top and the girls at the bottom of the jungle gym?

In much of childhood, girls make little distinction between their activities and boys' activities. Girls still compete with boys, and struggle to find their place on a higher rung, much as do the boys. Yet boys, from early childhood, do make distinctions between their activities and girls' activities. By the age of five, most boys have learned to avoid that which is associated with being a girl. They already know that they want to be men and that anything which does not move them toward that goal is the province of the "sissy," a category male children will do anything to avoid.

The desire to be masculine is encouraged in boys by the culture, by the mass media, and by their own families. But the strongest pressures toward an early assumption of masculinity come from males within the society. Fathers, for example, are more concerned with their boys being "real boys" than are their mothers. It was the father of my daughter's young male friend, not the mother, who decided his son at nine years of age was too old to play with a girl. Thus Deborah lost one of her best friends and moped around the house while the boy dutifully went to football games with his father.

Boys have, therefore, already retreated from girls' activities. Girls begin their retreat from boys' activities much later and more gradually. Although girls have been hearing, since they were little, that they are to grow up and care for others, that the world of achievement is not for them, that men and their accomplishments usually come first, this does not affect their behavior until they approach adolescence. The process of learning begins early when television shows, magazines, and books depict girls in interpersonal tasks and boys in achievement-oriented roles. Yet, all these messages appear to fall upon deaf ears until girls begin to look forward to romantic relationships. Then they decline to play football, downplay their achievements, and learn to cheer on the boys. For some girls this occurs early and for others late. I have seen one eight-year-old do this very well. For other girls, the realization of their feminine role does not occur until they are twelve to sixteen.

My daughter was one of those who came late to the realization of femaleness as separate from humanness. Raised in our household, she assumed that she had the same opportunities that everyone else had—and it was this assumption, in part, which brought about some of her difficulties. One incident is illustrative of her point of view throughout childhood. At about ten years of age, she was watching our occasional housekeeper finish her tasks so she could hurry home. Deborah asked her why she was in such a hurry. Peggy, our housekeeper, answered that she had to cook dinner for her husband and must not keep him waiting. The rest of the short dialogue was as follows:

Deborah: "How come you let your husband boss you around?"

Peggy: "I always let him do that, Debbie, that's the way it is."

Deborah (in exasperation): "Peggy! Don't you know anything about sex roles?"

Obviously my daughter had missed several lessons in the realities of the world.

Deborah's thoughts and dreams during this period reflected her rather nonsexist stance in the world. They were the views of a girl who came to a realization of femaleness later in adolescence and are thus reflective, to a certain extent, of the experience of childhood as opposed to girlhood. Yet her tendency to fantasize, to verbalize, to think about people as opposed to things was more in the feminine model than she might have liked to think at that age. So, yes, boys and girls do have differing experiences in childhood, but for some this is more extreme than others.

To the extent that boys and girls differ from each other, boys will have more experience with the overt uses of power, and girls more experience with the forms of love. Yet, at this stage, love is just a step away from power. As girls become aware that society does not always encourage girls to be strong, they learn to mask their strength. They transmute their power into the appearance of warmth and good will. The girl learns, at one time or another, that her strength is supposed to be the strength of the underdog, the child's strength carried into womanhood, the ability to smile, to please, to care for, and in return, to be protected by those who appear stronger than she.

Both sexes are learning about power, whether overtly or covertly, whether their victory is to be their own achievement or to be vicariously experienced. Yet neither sex learns about genuine power—that ability to do, to share, to contribute—which must be intertwined with a compassion for all human beings. They are too young for this. They are too concerned with doing. Their thinking is too concrete, too categorical. Hence, they learn about a lesser form of power: power that is domination, winning, competing, often at another's expense. The same struggle, in different guises, goes on at both the top and the bottom of the jungle gym.

This behavior is appropriate for their time in life. Is it behavior that is appropriate for their later lives as well? Is it behavior that fits them for a functioning role in society? It is behavior which will at least allow them to survive in the outer world. Yet is it the best of all possible alternatives? What behaviors are required for full functioning in the world as we know it today?

GROWING UP: THE EXPECTATIONS OF OTHERS

We now live in a world in which almost all men will go to work, and over half of all women. Thus, a goodly portion of both sexes need to develop the characteristics which are valued by the workplace. Such characterisitics generally include independence, initiative, decisiveness, perseverance, and the ability to work with others. Men and women will not only work, but they will also raise the next generation. In the past, this has been primarily women's domain but, today more men are entering this world and contributing to the care of children. Thus, women and men both need to develop the characteristics which enable them to be caretakers of the young. These characteristics include understanding, empathy, responsiveness, patience, and a willingness, at times, to put the needs of others first. Many boys and girls will eventually live more satisfying lives if they have developed the capacities to both work and care for others, to be both powerful and loving.

Yet, both boys and girls will meet a world which expects them to be, at least as adults, very different from each other. Thus, our children must not only learn to be full human beings, but they must also be ready to cope with the perceptions and expectations of others. Still, both within and without us, many of the old sex-role expectations are alive and well. For example, women at work are often expected to be more responsive and considerate than their male colleagues. Brusqueness and authoritarianism at home are more readily tolerated in men than in their wives, girl friends, mothers, and sisters. Men at work are frequently expected to place more value on achievement than on friendships. Women at home are expected to live up to the role of "good mother," and "good wife." Even if we ourselves are full human beings, both powerful and loving, we live in a world in which, according to our sex, we are expected to be particularly powerful and less loving, or the reverse. Finally, of course, we are participants in this world of shared expectations, and some of the world's expectations must inevitably become our own.

Therefore, we might expect our girls to be more interpersonally skilled than our boys, but not at the expense of their ability to accomplish things. We might expect our girls to be more experienced in home and child care than our boys, but not as their only alternative. On the other hand, we might expect our boys to be more intent on skill development, but not at the expense of their ability to relate to people. We might also expect our boys to be able to offer others their protection when necessary, but not if they see themselves only as protectors and others as the protected. In short, we might expect our children to grow up as both powerful and loving people (regardless of sex) and yet develop the knowledge and the skills which will permit them to live well in what is still a sex-differentiated world. This is a fine line to draw and one which takes years of experience to draw well.

How do we help our children do this? In a large part, what our children become will depend on our vision of ourselves and the world. If we, as adults, can blend power and love, and can see both the potential and reality of human life, we can provide an environment in which our children have the capacity to do the same. If we view our lives, as well as our children's lives, as carefree adventures in the circle of love, then we are ignoring the realities of our world and theirs. We cannot help them move through the realities of power which we choose not to recognize. Yet if we view our lives, as well as our children's lives, as an interminable jungle gym, then we are narrowing our possibilities as well as theirs. We cannot help them move beyond the power struggles of childhood if we see all of life as just more of the same.

But if we ourselves can come to terms with the realities of our world as well as the changing nature of human po-tential—and the possibilities of full human development—then we may be able to help our children along the path, knowing that the pathway is not the goal, and the current experience is not the end result. We may be able to do so even if their pathways diverge from ours as they set their own course in life. Most of us have difficulty with this a good part of the time. Yet, if we are aware of all of this in moments, in the best of times, it may see us—and our chil-dren—through to an approximation of the ideal balance of power and love.

CHAPTER TWO

FROM THE TOP TO THE BOTTOM: THE EXPERIENCE OF ADOLESCENCE

From the childhood preoccupation with power the young adolescent moves to a preoccupation with love. From a perception bound to the objective world, with its steps, ladders, and hierarchical structures, the adolescents shift their perception to the subjective world, with its mountains and its whirlpools, its rushing streams and stagnant marshes. The new subjectivity opens up possibilities of romance and despair, of self-glorification and self-denigration unknown to the child of the year before. Frightened by change, yet excited by possibilities, adolescents swing from the top to the bottom, alternately ecstatic and worried, enthusiastic and upset. The pangs and joys of adolescence have set in.

This is one image of adolescence: passionate, moody, searching, and romantic. But our cultural portfolio is replete with other images of the adolescent. There is the image of the good boy and good girl: the star athlete and the homecoming queen who share their glory with those who cluster about them. There is, too, the image of the bad boy and bad girl: the addict and the pusher, the delinquent and the runaway, participants in the urban street scene. Our images of adolescence run the gamut of possibilities from the best to the worst. They do so, in part, because adolescence symbolizes for most adults the best of their dreams and the worst of their fears.

THE CHARACTERISTICS OF ADOLESCENCE

Adolescence is *potential*. As they move into their teen years, young people have the first opportunity to consciously shape their lives. They leave the protected world of elementary school for the choices and the chaos of junior and senior high schools. They meet new people in a larger sphere and make new friends. They make beginning explorations of their future adult roles and envision themselves as doctors and truckdrivers, lawyers and cabbies, salespersons and (sometimes) thieves. The promise of both good fortune and greater misery lies ahead of them. They are beginning the adventure that will lead into adulthood and through middle and old age.

Adolescence is *change*. The capacity to live an adult life, biologically and cognitively, matures at about the age of twelve. The physical changes which occur at puberty cause adolescents to reevaluate themselves, in part, because others respond to them so differently. A person in an adult body is not treated as a child. New possibilities are opened up in the world of social interaction. Cognitively, too, the adolescent matures and is able to perceive the inner world as well as the outer world of childhood. The capacity for fantasy takes full flight and the realms of imagination offer multitudinous alternatives. Although cognitively and biologically mature, emotionally, adolescents are still closer to childhood. Growing emotionally to adapt to the new changes is a tumultuous process and it gives rise to the many images of adolescence.

Adolescence is *aloneness*. Unlike children, who explore the world of power against the secure backdrop of the family, adolescents recognize that they are different from their family. They are beginning the process of separation. They are aware that finally they must leave their parents and create their own family. What has been given will not always be theirs; some individual effort is demanded. With the awareness of distinction from parents and siblings, adolescents sometimes tremble on a precipice as they come to recognize their aloneness in what may be, at times, an overwhelming universe. This aloneness, this separation, is the preliminary step in finding self and, consequently, finding others. Yet it can be a frightening as well as an exhilarating experience.

Adolescence is *conflict*. With the awareness of separateness comes the recognition of contradictory emotional currents. One wants, after all, to grow up and make one's own decisions—and hence be alone. One wants, on the other hand, to remain a child and have all decisions made by another—and hence remain embedded in the family. One wants to be unique and loved, yet one fears being different and despised. One wants to be important and responsible and yet one is reluctant to fully accept the consequences of responsible action. The desire to grow up and the desire to "grow down" are the primary cross-currents in the conflict of adolescence.

THE TASK OF ADOLESCENCE: FINDING AN IDENTITY

In global terms, then, adolescence is potential, change, aloneness, and conflict. These four characteristics separate the adolescent from the child as if a voyage through outer space lay between the two. Part of the adolescent is still the child, and the adolescent will never totally leave the child behind. Part of the adolescent, also, is the emerging adult, and this inchoate maturity also lies within. If the tasks of childhood are, in general, to assess the outer world, to learn to map the external environment, with all its categories and labels, what then are the tasks of adolescence?

Inundated by biological, cognitive, and emotional change, the primary tasks of adolescence are to come to terms with this new internal world. The changes in physique, the new cognitive capacities for subjectivity, the heightened awareness of emotions, all prompt adolescents to turn inward. As Erik Erikson has stated, the adolescent's primary task is to find an identity. In doing so, adolescents come to know themselves and others in a more intensive way than ever before. They begin a period of self-questioning focused on the central question, "Who am I?" They explore their inner realm both by introspection and by watching their own images as reflected by others. How do others perceive me? What do *they* think? Do others like this new "me" that I am becoming? Adolescents are intensely self-conscious, particularly in the early teen years. They are beginning an assessment of self which is not only reflective of their inner experience but is reflected in the mirrors others hold up to them. (Adolescents often misinterpret these reflected images, in extremist fashion.)

As they become aware of themselves, they become aware of others in new ways. If I have an internal self, so then must others. If I think and feel, so then does he. There is a new awareness, not only of their own subjectivity but of the subjectivity of others. Consequently, in adolescence, young people can begin to see from another's eyes, to take another's viewpoint. Tied to the external categories of childhood, young people from the ages of six to twelve do not do this very well. In adolescence, however, the capacity for understanding and empathy begins to develop. Consequently, there is a new preoccupation with friendship, with knowing another person. Whereas childhood friends "do things" together, adolescent friends "find themselves" together. Still, the "finding myself and finding you" of mutual love must wait for a later era.

In all of this, there is also a romantic imaging of self and others. New capacities for fantasy shape both shining and tarnished images of self. The adolescent at one moment may gloat, "I am the most enlightened (strong, powerful, handsome, insightful) person of anybody I know." At other times, the same person may despair that "I am really nobody at all." This capacity for romantic imaging is not only turned on the self, but turned outward to others. They may alternately adore and despise: parents, friends, rock stars, political leaders, or people who live down the street. They may imagine someone to be (and truly believe it) the answer to all their dreams, the knight in shining armor, or the fair princess of gentle charms. They may also imagine that a person is the embodiment of every plague and fear, the destruction of every hope. Consequently, this is a time of best friends and worst friends wrapped into one. It is a time of passionate love and passionate hate. All of this, moreover, is not just imagined, not just thought, but experienced as real. It is felt. With this new capacity for imagination and fantasy, the adolescent can both soar and plummet.

THE DIFFERING EXPERIENCES OF ADOLESCENTS

Identity, friendship, and romantic love are the tasks of adolescence: to find oneself and to explore the images of others. Each adolescent is different: some emerge from adolescence with a sense of self and other, and an accompanying trust in both. Other adolescents come neither to know themselves nor others, but glide through adolescence, as through child-hood, with their eyes set on the outer world, not the inner. Immersed in the activities of their age group, they are un-aware that they and their world are changing. Numerous researchers[1] have pointed out that many adolescents do not face the challenges of this developmental period. They avoid the confrontation with their inner selves—and the inner selves of others. For them, adolescence is as childhood, a time of outward activity and inner quiescence.

SOCIAL CLASS

Some of the different experiences of adolescence can be traced to social class differences. Adolescents in the lower half of American society have a much sterner understanding of the outer realities. Many must help support their families early. Others are aware that they will begin to do so in mid- to late-adolescence as they leave high school. For these young people, adolescence is a time of gradual or not-so-gradual indoctrination into the adult world. This is not a free time, a space without responsibility, in which they may fantasize and dream. This is another step in a life course in which external realities offer little leeway for experimental departures. On the other hand, among the upper half of American society, one finds—in general—an openness to imagination and fantasy, because young people are generally unfettered by adult responsibilities. This is a time to dream and to experiment. This is a time to introspect and to project images into the future. Although adolescents in all circumstances do this, it is an experience more common to some social strata than to others.

[1] See Elizabeth Douvan and Joseph Adelson, *The Adolescent Experience*, Wiley, 1966.

GENDER

Some of the different experiences of adolescence are related to sex differences. Girls are more often dreamers than boys. Yet, in past eras, the content of boys' and girls' dreams also differed. Girls were (and many still are) much more prone to romantic fantasy and less enthralled by projections of competence. They define themselves less apart from others. Rather, their fantasies and their imaginations are often related to their interpersonal world, to being liked, loved, and adored, not to being innovative, competent, and achieving. Thus girls not only think about feelings more than do boys, but they center these feelings on a world in which others exist—a world in which the dreamer is often central.

I write here partly from the literature on adolescence but largely from my own experience. In an era prior to the women's movement, I spent my early adolescence in webs of fantasy: one day glowingly whisked along by my romantic hero to a school prom, another day, torn between world flights with another hero and responsibilities at home. Sometimes, I imagined conversations with characters from the 1800s: I would explain my world to them with all its romantic entanglements. In reality, of course, at thirteen, I did none of this. It seems from a distance that from eleven to thirteen I spent most of my time lying on my bed, reading, listening to records, and secretly choreographing dances to be performed under the lights somewhere. My chief companion of those years was another lonesome girl, a convenient but slightly dull friend.

If my daughter—in this age of surface liberation—has flights of romantic fantasy, I do not know. I suspect she might but I am not privy to them. A page of writing left about the house when she had just turned eleven reflected her first plunge into introspection. Very different from her earlier writings, this scrap from her notebook reflected a new subjectivity and a heightened awareness of self. It reflected not only awareness but displeasure with this awareness. She looked at herself and was not pleased—at least at the moment. Part of this self-exploration follows:

> I'm lazy, I eat too much. I boss people around a lot more than I should . . . I'm just wasting my life. I brag a lot too. One more thing I do wrong. I have too much self-pity. . . .
>
> Another thing I "do wrong" is I tattle-tale too much in class. Lots of people cheat in our class, and quite a few of them think it's cool to cheat. I tell on them and they get real mad at me. Johnny lies his head off just to try to get me into trouble. I guess it's because I've gotten him into trouble lots of times too. Maybe it would be better if I told on the times when I really thought it was necessary instead of times when it was only a little thing that didn't really matter. There's one thing I've found out though. The kids that cheat won't tell on the kids that cheat. . . .
>
> When I was halfway through writing this I got a good look at my life. I realized how it would feel to be the other person looking at me. I think I finally know how to change my life so it will be better for me and the people around me.
>
> Another thing I do wrong. I talk too much, and I try and get attention focused on me. I want people to care about my feelings though I do not care about theirs. I try and be like other people in order to have friends, but the best thing to do is to act myself. Another thing is I'm a poor loser. I make a big deal over nothing. . . .
>
> I'm just about over- everything. Such as over-help, -eat, -brag, -bossy, etc.
>
> I think my whole life is changing.

The themes of change, aloneness, and conflict are reflected in the self-questioning and self-criticism of my daughter at this age. They are the themes of male adolescence as well, yet the context in which they are expressed is very different. Boys, unlike girls, tend to focus more on who they will be, rather than who they will be with. Piaget said that it was amazing how many young adolescent boys were picturing themselves as the general marshall of France.[2] In our country, I suspect they imagine themselves as President. Alternative images are football heroes, daring airplane pilots, great scientists, and doctors who save the world. Many of my adult male friends express fantasies and dreams that are less people-centered than my own. They are more often filled with objects, actions, and unidentified faces than are mine. Most of their fantasies involve *doing* something, rather than *being* with someone. I think, also, they fantasize less and do more. They go out in the world in adolescence and fight to be strongest, best, and—in intellectual crowds—witty and bright. For boys, raised in our culture, love follows from doing; it is not sought for itself.

The result is that girls, who tend to mature earlier than boys, may have outdistanced their male peers by middle to late adolescence, because they have experienced more in terms of people than have boys. They have more interpersonal skills, more social graces, are more able to put someone else at ease than is a boy. Yet, by the time young people enter adulthood, boys have higher marks for maturity than do girls.[3] Struggling more with self alone during adolescence, boys come to terms with their own capacities for participation in the outer world. Based on this self-awareness, they later (in late adolescence and early adulthood) develop the interpersonal skills which carry their sense of competence into the outer world. Somehow, girls fall behind during the late teen years. Their early romantic fantasies

[2] Jean Piaget, *Six Psychological Studies* (New York: Vintage, 1968), p. 66.
[3] Anne Constantinople, An Eriksonian Measure of Personality Development in College Students, *Developmental Psychology*, 1 (1969), 357–72.

propel them into acquisition of social skills. They learn to be with others but not with themselves. On the other hand, boys have more opportunity to come to terms with self during adolescence and are not sorely handicapped by their later acquisition of interpersonal capacities.

The task of finding an identity is thus more often achieved by boys who, by the end of adolescence, have created a template of their future occupational goals, one which they may either measure up to, or fall short of, in their later lives. Yet, in so doing, boys develop a sense of who they are in relation to a work-oriented society. Girls, on the other hand, explore the world of friendship more than boys, but the future world of work less so. In terms of achievement, or future achievement, girls learn to prepare for a vicarious victory. Even today, when young women plan for both marriage and career they are more knowledgeable and realistic about the former than the latter. Girls, in contrast to boys, emphasize friendship and romance over self-knowledge during the years of adolescence.

The real sense of "finding oneself" may occur later for girls—far past the actual years of adolescence. In the last twenty years we have seen a wave of women "finding themselves" in their twenties and thirties. Suddenly, after marriage and children, they ask "Who am I?" The answer, when they find it, often shakes the structure of their lives in ways which they did not anticipate. Developmentally, the answer comes late, because as young girls they focused on love rather than power.

Thus the subjective influence of adolescence is seen more clearly in girls than boys. Females have permission to be more open in their explorations of the interpersonal arena. In childhood, the emphasis on love is more clearly expressed by girls. Yet both sexes, whether in covert or overt manner, experience the force of the predominant modality in both childhood and adolescence. Regardless of sex, children—secure in their families—explore the world of power. As adolescents, these slightly older people, aware of the first hint of separation, explore with a new urgency the world of love.

ATTITUDES TOWARD ADOLESCENTS

When I ask older adolescents in my college classes what matters most to them, young people of both sexes are very clear in stating that friendship and romantic attachments come first. Of both of these—friendship and love—they feel they have too little. Awakened by the first touch of aloneness, they yearn for connection. Aware of growing separation from their parents, they yearn to lose this sense of separation in relationship with another. It is perhaps the same drive which propels the later adolescent into love relationships which sends the younger adolescent in search of groups to which he can belong. Aware for the first time in their lives that they might be alone, they seek to submerge this sense by being with others.

Thus, we find young adolescents (as well as older ones) collected en masse in schoolyards, in parks, at rock concerts, at fast-food restaurants. They gather together, it seems, to lose their growing sense of differentness and aloneness. Yet they yearn for independence. They seek that sense of independence from their parents, if only in surface behavior, so they can lose it with their own kind. The gathering of the young in the same spot, the very numbers of them, the distinct clothing and hairstyles which show how different they are from the previous generation, the loud noise and the fast music which proclaim their distinction from the very young and the very old (anyone over twenty-one), is part of the phenomenon which gives rise to the dreams and fears of adults as they watch the adolescent world. There are so many of them and their behavior is so flagrant! How can one not both fear and envy them?

Adults do both fear and envy adolescents. Opinions about adolescents are more emotionally charged than opinions about any other age group. Adolescents are, at once, romanticized and disparaged. They are seen as both the best and the worst of the human race. Why do we come to rest our images, our hopes and our dreams, on such a motley crew of inexperienced folk? To explain this, we must return to the qualities which adolescence symbolizes. Adolescence symbolizes potential, change, aloneness, and conflict. Adolescence is, above all, a time of promise. As adults, however, we have to some degree, sullied our own youthful promise. Whether or not we have lived up to our dreams, we have—by living them out—limited them. We have rejected some options and chosen others. We have in the process injected inevitable imperfection into the possibility of our youth. When we look at youth we measure ourselves against our own dreams—and inevitably, to some extent, we see that we have failed to live up to these dreams.

Sometimes, we think, if we could do it over again, we might have chosen differently. Yet, as we watch young people live our lives again, they seem to do it so badly. They do not make their decisions with the adult wisdom that we might give them. They do not want, usually, the benefit of adult wisdom—such as it is. Rather, they make their decisions with the same shortsightedness we did when we were their age; we watch as they make the choices that, in moments of despair and resignation, we regret.

So we glorify the possibilities of adolescence and, seeing its limitations, we vilify the actuality. Yet there are young people, as there are older people, who do both well and badly with the opportunities they are given. There are people of all ages who respond to the possibilities of choice, risk making commitments, and learn from their mistakes. There are many adults, as well as adolescents, who turn from change and opportunity and attempt to continue as they are, failing to recognize that not to grow is to begin to die. In many ways, the behavior patterns of adolescence are the beginning of the adult journey. Yet, these patterns do not represent an unerring choice of a final direction, but are only the first attempts to establish tracks in the wilderness. Whether adolescents live up to the promise of creation, fall by the wayside, or tread previously well-worn trails, this is only an indication of later choices, and not the choice itself.

The behavior of adolescents is thus colored by adult perceptions, by adult hopes and disappointments, adult successes and failures. But for adolescents themselves, the immediate perception of life may be equally glorious or dismal for quite different reasons. Young people cluster together seeking to find a similarity that belies change, a togetherness that assuages aloneness, and a unity that denies conflict. They believe that they are finding meaning in each other and in the rituals of their age. Yet what they find, at least in the early years, are only images of themselves. They cannot reach each other in the way they can a few years hence. What they see is the projection of self. Their reflected images are alternately heartening and disappointing and they experience, in mirrors, both ecstasy and despair. Exposure to this world of mirrors may provide enough information from many vantage points so that later development may bring the integration which adolescents seek, but which is still out of reach.

CHAPTER THREE

CHANGE AND CONTINUITY: THE ADVENTURE OF ADULTHOOD

Our images of adulthood are very different from those of adolescence. While we see the adolescent as passionate, moody, searching and romantic, we often see the adult as controlled, stable, rational—and sometimes boring. Yet the process of being an adult is very much the same as the process of being an adolescent. At all stages of human life there is both change and continuity. At each stage, individuals face the question of integrating new experiences into their way of being and arriving at a higher level of development, or of rejecting those experiences and seeking to maintain the form of an earlier time. Each stage of life, therefore, represents a continuity with the past, an adaptation to changing circumstances in the present, and a projection of hopes and wishes into the future.

Conceptually, however, we tend to neglect the interplay of continuity and change throughout life. We see the adolescent as changing. We ignore the fact that adolescents are building on the experiences they have had in the past—in childhood. We see the adult, on the other hand, as never changing at all. We ignore the fact that adults move forward and retreat, cope with new developmental issues, and sometimes change their life circumstances dramatically. In this chapter, we will emphasize the dual themes of change and continuity, explore the various issues of adult development, and then question the degree of change and continuity in the lives of adults.

THE INTEGRATION OF CHANGE AND CONTINUITY: A LIFELONG JOURNEY

Change is central to the human experience. Biologically, we are all changing at every moment: even on the cellular level, we do not remain the same from one instant to another. Psychologically, we are also in flux: We all recognize the fact that we are up one moment, down the next, and sometimes happily in-between. In our relationships with others, moreover, we are always changing: Many psychologists have pointed out that relationships are either growing or dying; they do not remain the same. We are either investing energy in a relationship and thus continually revitalizing it, or it is dwindling away. Finally, we live in an era of great societal change in which our social, political, technological and ecological environment is markedly different from one year to the next. It is imperative that we develop a view of human beings which recognizes and plans for the biological, psychological, and social change which is occurring within and without.

Such a recognition of change does not, however, preclude the simultaneous recognition of continuity in individual lives and common threads throughout the human experience. We are all, to some extent, products of our personal and cultural history. We have our past experience upon which to build; even our changing behaviors shape themselves to patterns which have arisen in the past. All human beings share, to some extent, a common history and a common experience. We are similar biological organisms, with similar repertoires of psychological reactions, and we live within the same world. Out of our own pasts, therefore, we find a continuity of experience. Out of the commonality of all human experience, we find similarities with other human beings, which are the foundation of an empathic relationship with others. The continuity exists along with the recognition of change. The commonality exists side by side with the recognition of differentness. We are both changing and continuous. We are both different from others and yet similar. The polarities of human life exist both in ourselves and in our world. These polarities need not pull us apart, but can complement each other in the maturity of integration.

In fact, each stage of life pushes us to a new level of integration. At each stage of life, we are faced with a new set of polarities which pull us in different directions until we find the vantage point of integration, the point at which the currents begin to move in the same direction. The polarities we encounter at each stage are different manifestations of the need for change and continuity. They are also different expressions of our search for new balances of power and love. Or, they may be interpreted—as they are by Daniel Levinson as different expressions of the young/old polarities.[1] In other words, what is needed at each stage of life is a new balance between what is young (enthusiasm, passion, excitement) and what is old (experience, wisdom, responsibility). An eighty-year-old will seek to enliven the wisdom of old age with some of the spirited enthusiasm of youth, whereas a fifteen-year-old will stretch to reach a degree of understanding and responsibility to balance the passion of adolescence. Although the process of seeking this balance is very much the same at fifteen or eighty, the par-

[1] Daniel Levinson, *The Seasons of a Man's Life* (New York: Knopf, 1978).

ticular balance which is sought will differ. The content varies with the tasks required of persons at each successive stage of life.

THE FIRST HALF OF LIFE

In reviewing the varied tasks which we meet throughout adulthood, we begin, briefly, with adolescence, for the potential of adulthood is first seen in adolescence. Yet the potential rarely becomes an actuality at this preliminary stage. The adolescents facing questions of identity and intimacy make only initial steps in the process of actually finding themselves and coming to know another. Little is resolved in adolescence, although the beginning steps are undertaken. The process of resolution instead begins a decade later, as individuals come to terms with the realities of the outer world.

Identity and intimacy are, thus, the issues of the twenties, just as they were during adolescence. But these tasks are encountered on the testing ground of reality, where more weighty penalties follow mistakes. In the apprenticeship of adolescence, a lost job means a little less extra money, and a shattered relationship may mean a few months of heartache. In the twenties, the consequences may be unemployment, foreclosed mortgages, divorces and custody battles for young children. The penalties are higher for young adults than for adolescents, but so are the satisfactions. A boy may achieve good grades and enough money for a new car for resolving his conflict with the immediate world. A man in his twenties will reap, instead, a solid marriage, a healthy child, and job promotions which promise exciting challenges in the future. The heightened consequences of action when individuals move into young adulthood thus increase the necessity for resolution of conflicts around self and other. During the twenties young people firm up their commitments to occupations and to interpersonal relationships. They explore the real world and experience their first commitments in both work (power) and love.

In one's thirties, these commitments are tested and brought to new fruition. Whether in work or love (and sometimes both), the growing individual moves along the course laid down in the decade before. For men, this has often been the time of greatest immersion in work. For women, this has generally been the period in which there is the greatest investment in child-rearing. For men and women who work and raise children, this is a time of stress and overload, since our growth patterns in both occupational and family settings require a heavy investment of time and energies in both spheres of work and of love.

The end of the thirties often brings a close to this period of intense activity and opens the door for a period of reevaluation. The first half of life has been completed and some summing up of the past precedes the next leap into the future. The summing up has traditionally been different for men and for women. By age forty, most men have either "made it" or not "made it" in terms of their careers. As Levinson points out, successful men must come to terms with the fact that success does not mean much and unsuccessful men must accept the fact that their failure in conventional terms is not catastrophic. For all men, therefore, this period marks a reevaluation of past efforts in order to develop a greater breadth in new and future endeavors. For women at work, the pattern may be similar depending on the time of entrance into the job market. For women at home, this is generally a time of evaluating and summing up their child-rearing effort. The children are now gone, and they have half a lifetime left. Like men, women at midlife are asking, "What next?"

It is not just work and children which are subject to reevaluation at this time of life. One's interpersonal relationships, one's marriage and love life, are also subject to scrutiny. For marriages in which the men have been primarily tied to their work and women to their children (during their thirties), there is a recognition of the separation which this immersion in separate worlds has caused. Many men and women in their late thirties wonder if, indeed, they still recognize this person whom they married, so intent has each partner been on the occupational and family tasks of this era.

For men and women who both work and care for children, the problem is different. They may, indeed, have shared their two worlds and thus maintained the common ground upon which they first met. Yet, the stress of maintaining both worlds may have encouraged them to spend more time in *doing* and less time in *being*, particularly with each other. Thus, these individuals too may find that a communication gap has developed during their thirties which they may or may not bridge in their forties. Energy is freed from past activities which may be used to revitalize continuing relationships or to seek other interpersonal adventures. Once again, as in adolescence, there is the potential for much good to be wrought from this time of transition. Yet, this is still potential, not actuality.

THE SECOND HALF OF LIFE

The second half of life begins with a reevaluation of the first half. For many, it is the beginning of a realization that work and children are not the sum total of life. It is, in many respects, a reawakening to the multifaceted possibilities of human experience. Carl Jung has pointed out that this is a period of spiritual renewal.[2] Daniel Levinson speaks of the forties as a "second adolescence". Regardless of terminology, the forties is both an ending of the narrow work and family orientation of the recent past, and the beginning of a new adventure. This adventure, however, is not just shaped by the past, but by the vision of the suddenly diminishing future. The forties brings the first strong awareness that there is an end to the journey, that life is not forever, and that we will all die sooner than we might choose. This lends a certain urgency to the reawakening of the forties. The newly released energy-seeking adventure combines with the awareness that this energy is not infinite. Thus, the issue of death and rebirth sharpens the issues presented by other polarities. The forties thus both challenges past integrations and holds out the promise of deeper and broader integrations of the future.

The turbulence thus experienced by people at midlife may lead to either resignation and emptiness, or a new vitality and fullness of living. The integrations of the forties which is followed by the serenity of the fifties, see an individual through the despair preceding the wisdom and integration of the sixties, seventies, and eighties. Those who live through the entire journey experiencing the fullness of their conflicts as well as their resolutions, reach a wisdom, understanding, and compassion which is not possible for those who have not yet gone the full course. The end of the journey is then marked by wisdom and, at the same time, the enthusiasm of a youthful spirit.

The life cycle is, therefore, a continual balancing of young and old, enthusiasm and maturity, dream and reality. At each stage, too the dimension of either love or power predominates. Childhood explorations of power yield to

[2] Carl Jung, "The Stages of Life," in *The Portable Jung*, Joseph Campbell, ed. (New York: Viking, 1971), pp. 3–22.

adolescent preoccupations with love. Young adults intent on doing things are immersed in the world of power. The reawakening in the forties ushers in another era in which the awareness of love is once again intensified, a prelude to the integrations which will then occur in later life as individuals bring the two together. In this view, life is a process of continual challenge with increasing opportunities for hierarchical integration of new polarities. At the end of the journey lies the promise of full human development, which is manifest in those who have learned to blend justice and mercy, who have earned the right to say "yes" and the capacity to say "no," and who have developed both breadth of knowledge and depth of insight. The old have the opportunity which is denied the young; they reap the benefits of a full integration of the spheres of love and power.

THE DISTINCTIONS BETWEEN MEN'S AND WOMEN'S LIVES

At the end of the journey, as at the beginning, the integration of love and power may hold out its promise for both men and women. In old age, as in early childhood, there may not be startling differences between the sexes. Yet, in terms of love and power, for most of life's journey, there are distinctions between men and women. During most of their lifetime, men and women move toward the goal of integrating love and power on differing tracks with differing timetables. Men have been groomed for the world of power, and women trained in the sphere of love. In their early years, they develop disparate perspectives and come to stand in different places as they begin their adult journey. The differences learned in childhood are given new meaning as both sexes face the reevaluation of midlife.

Men, who learn the rules of power early, often find by

their late thirties or early forties that power is insufficient as a foundation for a satisfactory life. Thus, the midlife crisis for men is often prompted by the need to integrate their potential for love with their experience of power. Levinson calls this time of life a second romantic period in which feelings, emotions, and impulses come to the surface. Much of this new emotional expression may appear to be a destructive eruption rather than a creative integration. Indeed, in the process of transition, it is likely that this is so. Few of us can use new capacities with balance or with grace; the testing of new behaviors takes practice to overcome our clumsiness. Thus, the midlife crisis is often an explosion of emotion and what may be regarded as "irrational behavior". Yet, the promise of a new and higher level of integration is often realized after traversing what appears to be a difficult path.

For women, the integration of love and power looks rather different at midlife. Women, who have been taught to depend on love, come later than men to a realization of their own power, often in the late twenties and thirties. Thus, many women who have been primarily raising children are once again found in educational institutions and business organizations. At thirty to thirty-five, they are exploring their potential for action in the world. This exploration of power by women is often threatening to the men who watch them, and sometimes justly so, for not only does woman's newly found power challenge the male's desire for stability and supremacy, but women also may not be using their newly discovered capacities with the greatest degree of finesse. Like men learning to love, women growing in power may stumble along the path. Yet, once again, this path must be traversed if we are to grow as full human beings using the breadth and depth of our human potential.

Culturally, the separation of love and power may be viable for men and women until midlife. This separation implies, however, that men who need to be both powerful and loving will tend to use what they know about power to gain love. Similarly, women will tend to use love to gain power. Thus, it is unlikely that any of us will have emerged from our early socialization without learning both to separate and to confuse love and power. The increasing opportunities for choice as individuals are released from the commitments of the twenties and thirties, however, prompts both men and women to regain that which has been previously set aside. For some, the challenge is too great and they continue the second half of their lives with lowered vitality and a degree of resignation. For others, the promised integration is achieved, and the second half of life is a great adventure undertaken with enthusiasm.

The final integration brings together all the differentiated potentials of human beings. Yet, as in all adventures, there are dangers along the way. At each level of new integration, we risk losing what we have in order to bring into being what we have not. What happens, however, is that when we have taken the next step, we have not lost what we had, but rather blended the past with the present and with our future potential. Still, along the way, the new integration is never guaranteed—so the adventure of living is experienced in both its threatening (loss of the old) and promising (creation of the new) aspects.

YOUTH VERSUS OLD AGE

Is the process of living such an exhilarating experience? There is some evidence that it is, as well as much evidence that it is not. If youth is not much different from old age, is it possible that they are both more dreary than has been portrayed? Or, on the other hand, is youth really a different time, full of promise, that stands in stark contrast to the resignation of old age?

Let us first examine the results of a research project completed by two of my university classes in the last year. One class completed life-experience interviews with 150 individuals from the ages of twelve to ninety-six. In the course of the interview, the students asked each individual to list the five most important personal events in their lives. The other class then analyzed the interviews.[3] First, individuals in each decade of life, from adolescence through the fifties, were grouped together. Individuals over sixty, regardless of age, were analyzed as one group. Then, for each group of individuals, classified by age, the major personal events were sorted into categories and identified by the age period in which they occurred.

The categories which were most significant were similar across age groups for both men and women. In terms of personal importance, events revolving around family issues held first place. Marriage and birth of the children were listed by almost all individuals. The next major category, which came in a distant second, was job related. In particular, individuals mentioned first jobs, or the beginning of work at a certain place as important. This was more often true for men than for women. There was one notable exception to this ranking of family first and occupation second. For men who had lived through the first and second world wars (but not Korea or Vietnam), their war experience was marked as the most significant event in their lives. In short, women emphasized family issues throughout, and men emphasized war experiences (if they occurred), family landmarks, and occupational events in a review of their past lives.

Most of the events listed marked beginnings in their

[3] Appreciation is due the students who compiled the data from these interviews. They are Bill Brewis, Carol (Valchine) Brewis, Richard Chiola, Jacqueline Kyler, Paul Paczkowski, Beatrice Roehr, and Doug Webster.

lives; some of them marked endings. When they were classified according to the decade in the individual's life when
they occurred, a clear pattern emerged. For all individuals
beyond adolescence, almost every age group (from twenty
to sixty) said that the most important events in their lives
occurred primarily in their twenties. What they are saying,
it seems, is that they laid down the course for their lives in
their twenties. In the first decade of young adulthood, they
made important beginnings. If we assume, as I do, that important events signal major changes in a person's life, most
of these people made few such changes after their late twenties. Their lives were set in a significant way by the time
they were thirty. They had assumed jobs, married, and had
children. These events provided the forms in which they
continued their lives, many quite happily, until old age.

At this point, judging from the people over sixty, new
events loomed large which were related to the deterioration
of life. These events marked endings. These findings suggest
that a full and exciting adulthood, marked by new challenges, was not the lot of this sample. The major fruits of
adulthood were borne in the twenties, little happened of
significance until late in life when death began to take its
toll.

For another look at the question of youth versus old
age, we might examine the words of psychologist Carl Rogers, writing of his life between sixty-five and seventy-five:

> ... for me this has been a fascinating ten years—full of ad-
> venturesome undertakings. I have been able to open myself
> to new ideas, new feelings, new experiences, new risks. In-
> creasingly I discover that being alive involves taking a
> chance, acting on less than certainty, engaging with life ...
>
> As I consider all the decades of my existence there is only
> one other ... which can be compared to this one. It too in-
> volved risk, learning, personal growth, and enrichment. But

it was also a period of deep personal insecurity and strenuous professional struggle, much more difficult than these past years. So I am being honest when I say that all in all, this has been the most satisfying decade in my life . . .

As a boy I was rather sickly, and my parents have told me that it was predicted I would die young. This prediction has been proven completely wrong in one sense, but has come profoundly true in another sense. I think it is correct that I will never live to be old. So now I agree with the prediction. I believe that I will die young.[4]

Why, for Rogers, is life so exciting when for many others of his age, death and illness are the primary events? Rogers speaks of the willingness to risk, to "gamble on something new." Whether he succeeds or fails, he says, learning is garnered from the experience. The willingness to risk is central to his view of life. In the same article he writes:

All . . . [that I do] brings change, and for me the process of change is life. I realize that if I were stable and steady and static, I would be a living death. So I accept confusion and uncertainty and fear and emotional highs and lows because they are the price I willingly pay for a flowing, perplexing, exciting life.[5]

We might conclude that there are many pathways through adulthood. Along each pathway, there are many stopping places. A few, such as Carl Rogers, buy a ticket for the full ride. Others are on the journey only for a while, and after the first adventure have had their fill. Is this a question of outward circumstances or inner choice? In part, it must be outward circumstances. Carl Rogers says he has been lucky in his marriage, his work, his friends, and his health. Yet

[4] Carl Rogers, Growing Older or Older and Growing, *Journal of Humanistic Psychology*, 1980, *20* (4), p. 5–16.
[5] *Ibid.*

this cannot be the complete answer, for there are many others who enjoy the same good fortune and yet do not take the chances of making new beginnings after the middle of life. Perhaps this is as it ought to be, for we come into this world with different hopes and different dreams, and perhaps we live them out in very different ways.

We may speculate that those of our elders who continue to venture are given courage and support by a continually renewed experience of both power and love. The fresh experience of power is the foundation from which courage springs. The fresh experience of love is the foundation of faith in self and others. In contrast, those who stop along the way are recycling past experiences of power and love and are prey to the lack of vitality that comes with drawing on the old and avoiding the new. This is, however, speculation. There is still no resolution to the questions on youth and age. Is aging a process of slowly dying or of increasing wisdom and enthusiasm? It can be both. The verdict for most of us is not in.

CHAPTER FOUR

THE HIGH ROAD AND THE LOW ROAD: DEVELOPMENTAL PATHS OF MEN AND WOMEN

The balance of love and power and the potential for integration varies throughout the life cycle. We have noted that children are preoccupied with power, adolescents with love, and the emphasis on productivity in the early adult years gives way, for some, to a renewed emphasis on intimacy at midlife, a prelude to the final integration of the later years. Yet if we survey those who have traveled the full journey and arrived at high levels of integration in their later years, throughout recorded history there are more men than there are women. (As is well known, however, history has been written by men and may not therefore, represent an unbiased record of either male or female achievement.) Does the balance of love and power differ for men and women when they have come to the height of their development? Is there indeed a high road and a low road in the human journey, one traveled by men and one by women? A number of research studies, exploring the higher levels of development of men and women at varied ages, suggest that this is so.

AGENCY AND COMMUNION: SELF AND OTHER

A number of studies undertaken at the University of California at Berkeley reveal developmental differences in adult men and women. These researchers, led by Jack Block and Jeanne Block, interpret the differences in terms of "agency" and "communion," which is similar to our use of power and love.[1] Agency, they say, represents the masculine principle and is concerned with the self-protection, self-assertion and self-expansion of the organism. Communion represents the feminine principle and it describes the individual existing as part of a larger unit in relationships with others. The height of maturity, argue the Blocks, occurs when the two modalities—agency and communion—are integrated with each other. At this point, the self-assertiveness learned by men earlier is tempered by considerations of mutuality and interdependence; for women, the early learning of harmonious group skills is amended to include self-assertion and self-expression. These researchers point out, however, that this level of integration is achieved only by a few, since our current socialization practices "impede the development of mature ego functioning."

In one of their studies, two groups of men and women were distinguished in terms of their degree of socialization. Socialization was defined as the degree of warmth and control the parents demonstrated in their child rearing. A child who was raised with moderate controls and warm parents

[1] J. Block, A. von der Lilpe, and J. H. Block, "Sex-Role and Socialization Patterns: Some Personality Concommitants and Environmental Antecedents," *Journal of Consulting and Clinical Psychology,* 41 (1973), pp. 321–41; J. H. Block, "Conceptions of Sex Role: Some Cross-Cultural and Longitudinal Perspectives," *American Psychologist,* 28 (1973), pp. 512–26.

was considered highly socialized. A child who was either neglected or overprotected and who was sometimes rejected by the parents was considered poorly socialized.

In terms of other measures of maturity, the well-socialized men looked very good and the poorly socialized men fared badly. The well-socialized men in adulthood had combined the positive aspects of power and love, or agency and communion. Jeanne Block writes that they "were productive, effective, dependable, and conscientious." They were basically agentic (powerful) in orientation but had tempered this with respect for others. The authors conclude that socialization appears to expand life options for men; that is, the better socialized they were, the more opportunities they had in life.

Well-socialized women, on the other hand, were described as contented and conventional. They had forsaken achievement and autonomy. They were docile and responsive and occasionally anxious. Poorly socialized women, in contrast, were striving and achieving, yet deficient in interpersonal skills. In neither of these groups did one find the integration of power and love found in well-socialized men. The researchers comment that although socialization appears to expand life options for men, it narrows them for women. Our culture does not value independence in women and hence well-socialized women learn to renounce independence, which is a necessary ingredient of high levels of development. Jeanne Block concludes that "the achievement of higher levels of ego functioning for women is more difficult" than for men.

Men are thus raised to power but, by midlife, some have tempered this with love. Women are raised to love and, at midlife, are still encapsulated in the interpersonal world. It appears that for a man to be loving in our society is not as disastrous as for a woman to be powerful. Men are given the option of emotional expressiveness within the home if they choose to develop that capacity. Women have no arena in which they can, with full social acceptance, be overtly powerful. Hence socialization for men may be a blessing but for women a curse. However, lack of socialization is not a better alternative.

CRISIS AND COMMITMENT: MEASURING IDENTITY

A second set of studies, directed by Norma Haan[2] and Jeanne Block[3] assessed the developmental levels of college students in several areas. In general, they were interested in the degree of conflict in the family background of students with a strong ethical orientation. They found that moderate degrees of conflict marked the developmental history of the most highly developed, and that conflict was more important in the background of highly developed young women than young men. Yet, these authors came to a similar conclusion as did those of the first study: higher levels of development are more difficult for women to achieve than for men, and women who were highly ethical in this study did show more signs of stress than did their male counterparts.

Another body of research focuses on the achievement of an identity in young men and women. James Marcia initiated this work based on the theories of Erik Erikson, who

[2] N. Haan, M. B. Smith, and J. Block, "The Moral Reasoning of Young Adults: Political-Social Behavior, Family Background and Personality Correlates," *Journal of Personality and Social Psychology*, 10 (1968), pp. 183–210; N. Haan, "Moral Redefinition in Families as the Critical Aspect of the Generation Gap," *Youth and Society*, 3 (1971), pp. 259–83.

[3] J. Block, "Generation Continuity and Discontinuity in the Understanding of Societal Rejection," *Journal of Personality and Social Psychology*, 22 (1972), pp. 333–45.

defined the task of adolescence as finding an identity.[4] Identity, according to Erikson, presumes an integration of personal attributes in light of one's expected future role as a contributing member of adult society. The formation of identity, according to Erikson, is the prerequisite for intimacy and the capacity for love. Having attained the capacity for both constructive work and mutual love, one would suppose that one has also achieved a balance of agency and communion, or power and love.

Marcia was responsible for developing a scale that measures identity. He designed his scale into two major areas which he saw as components of identity. One area is "crisis", or the fact of having thoroughly thought through one's own perceptions due to internal conflict. The second is "commitment", or the capacity to devote oneself fully to beliefs, occupational goals, and eventually relationships. He divided college students he studied into four groups: those who scored high on both areas he termed "identity achievers"; those high on crisis and low on commitment he defined as "moratoriums"; those high on commitment and low on crisis were "foreclosures"; and those low on both crisis and commitment were termed "identity diffusions".

Among young men, Marcia found "identity achievers" were capable, self-confident, and flexible. They come from homes, Marcia suggested, in which the parents were both warm and moderately controlling. "Moratoriums", on the other hand, shared many of the achievement-oriented, flexible characteristics of the "identity-achievers", but were not content, happy, dependable, nor predictable. Their lives were in crisis. These people, Marcia implied, came from

[4] J. Marcia, "Development and Validation of Ego Identity Status," *Journal of Personality and Social Psychology, 3* (1966), pp. 551–58; J. Marcia, "Ego Identity" (unpublished manuscript, Simon Fraser University, 1976); J. Marcia, "Identity in Adolescence," in *Handbook of Adolescence*, J. E. Adelson, ed. (New York: Wiley Interscience, 1980), pp. 159–87.

homes in which control may have been a stronger factor than warmth.

Male "foreclosures", on the other hand, were rigid and authoritarian, as well as defensive and stereotyped, Marcia found. They came from warm, child-centered and accepting homes. Marcia suggested that perhaps the control dimension was negligible in these homes so that there had never been any need for these young men to seek their own identity and to define themselves against another. Finally, those labeled "identity diffusions" were uncommitted, unquestioning, and drifting, seeking merely to maintain their own survival and a minimal level of security. The parents of "identity diffusions" were often emotionally absent or hostile. Whereas "foreclosure" parents demonstrated more love than power, the parents of "identity diffusions" demonstrated too little of either.

In surveying the results of all these groups, it is apparent that—as assessed by other measures of emotional well-being—the more crisis in one's life, the better. In this view, crisis plus commitment leads to the highest level of maturity, but crisis without commitment comes closest to this level. Young men who are either "identity achievers" or "moratoriums" appear to offer promise of later high levels of development.

In turning to the women, however, Marcia and his colleagues found different patterns.[5] Where male "identity achievers" and male "moratoriums" appeared to be the most healthy on other measures, female "identity achievers" and female "foreclosures" scored highest on other measures of mental health. The unifying thread of "identity achievement" and "foreclosure" is commitment or stability. "Moratorium" and "identity diffusion" women were similar; nei-

[5] J. Marcia and M. L. Friedman, "Ego Identity Status in College Women," *Journal of Personality*, 38 (1970), pp. 249–63.

ther had a stable frame of reference for making decisions and this tended to impede their functioning much more than in the case of men.

The development of a stable frame of reference thus appears to be very important in the psychological lives of women. "Foreclosure" women take this frame of reference from their parents and are content. "Identity achievers" develop an internal frame of reference which gives them similar stability. However, it is notable that anxiety is higher in identity-achieving women than in "foreclosures". The implication is that the formation of identity for a woman is not socially approved and therefore is accompanied by a greater degree of internal conflict. On the other hand, "foreclosure" women, unlike their male peers, appear to be very healthy, although Marcia termed them childlike in many respects. The conclusion is similar to that cited earlier: well-socialized men expand and personalize their options whereas well-socialized women adapt to whatever system is handed to them. Once again, the prognosis for women, in a society dominated by masculine values, is poor.

A later study by one of Marcia's colleagues, Jacob Orlofsky, obtained similar results.[6] In his sample of college women, half of them were "foreclosures". His prognosis for identity achievement and high self-esteem in these women was poor. Orlofsky pointed out that it is most difficult for "foreclosure" women to break the parental mold and there is little reinforcement for such from society. He concluded that these findings "call into question the socialization process which requires that girls suppress or fail to properly learn the very [assertive and instrumental] behavior that leads to high self-esteem in males."

Each of these studies augurs poorly for the development

[6] J. Orlofsky, "Sex-Role Orientation, Identity Formation, and Self-Esteem in College Men and Women," *Sex Roles*, 6 (1977), pp. 561–66.

of high levels of maturity in women. High levels of development are defined by all these researchers—implicitly or explicitly—as the combination of power and love, or the characteristics associated with assertion and those associated with caring for others. Studies of adult men show that some men do achieve this integration. These same studies do not show the same results for women. Furthermore in younger samples, there is evidence that young men are working toward achieving this balance of love and power, whereas young women, in general, are not. Finally, those women who are achieving this balance are suffering the heightened levels of anxiety which ensue from combating the expectations of our culture.

By current standards of human development, it appears that women are consigned to the low road while men may tread the high road. Consequently, women have little opportunity to attain the heights that the best of men attain. Is this the end result of the process of little boys growing up and little girls growing down? Recently, there has been a new viewpoint on this question, which does not provide contradictory evidence, but challenges the cultural definition of high levels of human development.

HIGH DEVELOPMENT: A MASCULINE ORIENTATION

This point of view argues that our standards of high development have been particularly favorable to a masculine orientation. For example, we call those men "highly developed", who have been trained to live in a world of power, but who have learned to temper their actions with love. But does not power still dominate their thinking? Is not power first and love second in these men, just as it is in the value structure of Western culture? Perhaps our standards for high development are subtly biased toward the masculine. For example, we may talk about the integration of love and power but, when given human form, the final result is usually a lot of power and a little love, rather than a balance or the other way around.

In two separate papers, Carol Gilligan and Norma Haan suggest that this may be so. Gilligan argues that our models for high development are male and have been built on a belief in separateness which is incompatible with the socialization and belief systems of most women.[7] She suggests that there is another developmental path which is built around the concept of connectedness and is most highly evidenced in the lives of women. She says that this developmental pathway results in a high level of responsibility and care for others, which is evidenced in the lives of many mature women. Norman Haan, in a similar vein, argues for a system of interpersonal ethics as opposed to the more impersonal ethical system which researchers have traditionally associated with high development.[8] This interpersonal system of ethics forms a developmental system of its own, and is found more frequently in the thought and behavior of adolescent girls than adolescent boys. Both Gilligan and Haan say, in effect, that we have overlooked a parallel developmental system which grows from the feminine context, and have inappropriately measured women against a system which has been developed from the masculine context.

This may very well be true. The reason men do so well in terms of our models of development may be that we have built all our models on male images. If this is so, as it appears

[7] C. Gilligan, "In a Different Voice: Women's Conceptions of Self and Morality," *Harvard Educational Review, 17* (1977), pp. 481–517.

[8] N. Haan, "Two Moralities in Action Contexts: Relationships to Thought, Ego Regulation, and Development," *Journal of Personality and Social Psychology, 36* (1978), 286–305.

to be, then women will always fail to measure up. We may devise alternate systems in which women do better, as Gilligan and Haan have done. Yet, when we turn to the outer culture in which masculine values are predominant, the alternative models, competing with the more traditional ones in a larger system dominated by men, will always fail to measure up. Thus we are faced with two alternatives: the traditional one—in which women fail to achieve as well as men within the usual models of development; or the alternate choice of devising models—in which women do well, though these models fail to stand up to the traditional ones in terms of cultural effectiveness. If we are going to face the reality of our world, we must recognize the predominance of the male and the fact that, within systems designed by and for males, women will always be losers.

Still, there is victory even in losing. The lessons which are learned by those who are second are often more valuable than lessons learned by those who are first. The process of seeking to integrate love and power is the same for both men and women. The content of the achieved balance, however, will differ. In our world, the balance weighs more heavily on the side of power, at least for men. In women, however, the balance of power and love, when achieved, weighs heavier on the side of love. Although the world generally finds that this resolution has less merit, both women and men have the same intrinsic satisfaction which accrues from personal integration and resolution of personal struggles. Furthermore, the balance achieved by women, working side by side with men, may right the larger balance which men alone have set askew.

There are, however, other considerations. Men may rate more highly in terms of developmental maturity because the culture places a priority on masculine values. The consequences for men are not entirely beneficial. In all situations, we tend to put higher expectations and greater pressures on those who are expected to assume the thrones of power—whether or not they do. There is less latitude for deviance for those who are number one. In a general sense, this is true of men in our culture: they are expected from an early age to be "masculine," to achieve, and to stand on their own feet. The consequences of these expectations are that there are more psychological casualties in the early years among men than among women. There is less opportunity for men to explore a variety of alternatives, particularly if those alternatives smack of the feminine.

For women, on the other hand, there are more options. Some recent authors (for example, Maggie Scarf in *Unfinished Business*) deplore the fact that women's path is not straight and narrow, but fuzzy enough to cause confusion.[9] Yet, the source of the confusion is *choice*. In a number of areas, whether they are termed masculine or feminine, women have the opportunity to try new things and test their skills. As a consequence, in their early years, there are many less psychological casualties among females. Rather, it is in their adult years, when women find that it is difficult to excel at *any one thing* that the burdens of being female take their toll. There are benefits for both sexes, and there are difficulties; each has its own possibilities and pitfalls.

If we say that little boys grow up and take the high road and little girls grow down and take the low road, we must note that the assignation of high and low, up and down, is a cultural artifact, based on male assumptions about what is good and what is not. Men may continue to weigh the integrative balance in favor of power, and we would be much poorer if women did not weigh the integrative balance in favor of love. Yet, if neither sex gives up the struggle which carries them through the full journey of life, neither shall be the poorer. Nor shall anyone care how we choose to name the roads, be they high or low, on which we make our course.

[9] Maggie Scarf, *Unfinished Business* (Garden City, N.Y.: Doubleday, 1981).

PART II

MEN AND WOMEN IN RELATIONSHIP

CHAPTER FIVE

FULFILLING RELATIONSHIPS: VISION AND REVISION

The vision of fulfilling relationships involves the paradoxical nature of love: the fact that when we find ourselves at our strongest and most powerful we are able to transcend ourselves in communion with another. Individuals capable of such love experience their potency in the world, and a relationship between two such potent individuals increases the energy and vitality of both. The strength of one enhances, rather than depletes, the strength of the other, leading to the possibilities of genuine transcendence of self.

On the other hand, the reality of many relationships involves a lack of potency. What one gives to another, one takes from oneself; what one uses for oneself, one withholds from the other. In such relationships love and power are seen as opposites, and partners find they cannot stand alone but require the continuing security of the relationship in order to provide structure and security for their world.

Thus the vision of what we can be, when we examine our lives more fully, diverges from the reality of what we are. Our ideals and our realities often diverge, and if we are to live fully we must accept the imperfect reality in which we live without losing the vision of where we may someday be. In the process of living more fully the reality of our lives, we move incrementally closer to the vision of fulfilling human relationships, in which individuals combine both the strength and caring of power and love.[1]

EARLY VIEW: AUTONOMY AND OPEN COMMUNICATION

The above is a summary of views which I presented a few years ago. There were two assumptions about human beings and relationships which lay behind these views. The first assumption was that people are healthiest when they are strongly autonomous, that is, when they are able to live either alone or with others. The second assumption was that relationships are facilitated by open and transparent communication. Behind this second assumption were two other unstated ones: that verbal communication can clearly express what a person is thinking and feeling at a given moment, and that whether or not this communication is understood is the problem of the listener, not the speaker.

The two assumptions about autonomy and openness are necessarily intertwined. If we are straightforward about our own point of view without regard to that of our listener, then we risk losing the listener. Another person may not be willing to tolerate the impact of honest disclosures at any particular time and place. Therefore, those who risk open communication at all times must be prepared to be alone. In other words, they must be autonomous. Such a carefree belief in openness assumes that if I take care of myself in communication, you will take care of yourself. The result is that, in other areas of life, I may wind up taking care of myself while you take care of yourself.

[1] Barbara Forisha, "Fulfilling Relationships: The Vision and the Reality," *Journal of Humanistic Psychology, 18* (1978), pp. 69–73.

THE MYTH OF "MATURE AND REASONABLE PEOPLE"

I would argue now that my earlier vision of a fulfilling relationship, with its assumptions about autonomy and openness, misrepresents certain facts about human beings and their relationships. I have come to realize, that I took part in perpetuating what a friend of mine called the "myth of two mature, reasonable people in relationship with each other," or—for short—the "Mature and Reasonable" myth. Other friends of mine—marriage counselors—say that they are forever trying to disabuse young people of the "Prince Charming and Fair Maiden" myth. We all know that one: The Prince Charming myth has long roots in our culture. In recent years, however, it has been supplanted by the myth of the Mature and Reasonable Man and Woman. We have not, indeed, grown more mature and reasonable in recent years; rather, we have exchanged one fiction for another.

There are still some who would argue that Mature and Reasonable is not mythology, but truth. I have come to believe differently. None of us are flawless human beings; we all have blind spots, or areas in which we do not operate very well. Since we are all interdependent with others on this planet, any advocacy of autonomy must be seen in this context. There are times when we say things openly which are not at all "reasonable," no matter how enlightened we consider ourselves. If others, at those times, did not forgive us for our weakness, we could pay dearly for many remarks. Yet, at some level, other people recognize irrationality in themselves and others, and allow us to say *we won't* when we will and *we can't* when we can. That is, they do so if they are not swept away by a belief in the openness of mature and reasonable people.

74

LATER VIEW: INDIVIDUAL COMPLEXITY AND SEPARATE REALITIES

In the last few years, therefore, I have come to challenge my own early views, to reevaluate and to revise my concept of a fulfilling relationship. I have moved toward another view which focuses more on individual complexity and individual differences, and the need to understand the disparate realities of individuals in close connection with each other. The revised view emphasizes openness sometimes but not all the time. It recognizes that verbal communication reveals what we *think* we know at any given moment and thus it often expresses only a fragment of our experience. Nor does our immediate expression of an experience at a given moment in time particularly mesh with the framework of the one to whom we speak. The emphasis on complete openness is one-sided if there is no regard for the recipient of our verbal "fallout." Hence, in my current view, human beings are much more complex than I previously thought, and the complexity of not one, but two, must guide communication in a relationship.

In addition to recognizing the complexities of human beings in relationship to each other, I am more emphatic about the necessity of relationships for their own sake. In the last decade or so, we have oversold the concept of autonomy. Many of the greatest proponents of autonomy are also least able to make a commitment—and most of them live alone. As I have come to know myself better, I realize that I am happiest and most fulfilled living in relationship with others. I have also come to recognize and accept that a measure of autonomy is the necessary cost of relationship.

I have moved thus from vision to revision in my own beliefs about human beings and relationships. The transition occurred at the end of a brief but powerful relationship in my life, which I had entered fully believing in the myth of Mature and Reasonable People. I believed that if I were completely honest about my feelings at all times, and maintained a sense of my own autonomy, the relationship would prosper and grow. For many reasons, the relationship neither prospered nor grew—quite possibly for the long-term benefit of both parties. Yet when it ended I was forced to reevaluate my beliefs and to recognize that openness in communication and a defense of autonomy may serve only short-range goals at the expense of the relationship.

As a consequence, I have dramatically altered my views on open communication in relationships on autonomy, about which there will be further discussion later. In terms of communication, I have come to realize that I must spend as much time understanding another person's perspective as my own, and that the reality of a male friend, for example, will be as much a part of the communication as my own. For example, when I say, "It's cold out, and I'd like to go home," someone else may—because of his own past experience—interpret my statement as meaning "I don't want to be with you any more." It seems to me that in below freezing weather, late at night, after a long day, I am being Mature and Reasonable. To interpret that statement as rejection is to my way of thinking, obviously immature and unreasonable. Yet, *I am as responsible for the response as for the initial statement*, since the behavior engendered by the response will affect my own life through the relationship. If I do not account for the potential response, I am shortchanging the long-term health of the relationship.

Statements may be open and honest, mature and reasonable, or *not*; what matters is how those statements will be interpreted by the other person. Reasonableness and maturity are so strongly interwoven within individual frames of reference, that we might as well throw them out as a standard of behavior. Those frames of reference are very complex and sometimes subconscious: They will not be explained to anyone in twenty-five words or less.

Instead of responding to verbal statements I have come to focus on behavior. What people *do* can tell us more about themselves than what they say. While patterns of behavior often spring from genuine commitments and authentic beliefs, other times these behaviors spring from subconscious reactions to long-ago situations. When we articulate to others our beliefs and commitments, we may be understood as we understand ourselves, but too often our words are colored by past events in a way we ourselves may not realize, and we are susceptible to misinterpretation.

Our past experience emerges to shape our communication when we are in close relationship with another, and vital issues (such as our self-esteem) are at stake. At such times, we may begin to respond to events in our own past—rather than to what is happening in the present. To the ears of others, we may then say the strangest things. This experience is sometimes true for all of us and is the major deterrent to being Mature and Reasonable. We all have trigger points which have been shaped by our personal history. We need to understand the past experience of another person to know why, "It's cold outside and I want to go in," is interpreted as "You don't want to be with me any more." When we understand the frames of reference, we can understand the logic of the seemingly unreasonable statement. Within the appropriate frame of reference, most statements become reasonable.

A PERSONAL TRANSITION: EXCERPTS FROM LETTERS

The slow transition in my own life, discarding my belief that open and honest communication was the foundation of a fulfilling relationship is chronicled in personal letters from that period. Excerpts from letters written at the end of the previously mentioned relationship, indicate the ways in which I fight change, the slowness of transition, and the possibilities of reformulating a more viable view of life and relationships. The result, for me, was an end to the Mature and Reasonable People myth.

I began the relationship by strongly believing in this myth. In the early letters, you will note, I am clearly Mature and Reasonable. We have just had what I viewed as a small altercation which resulted in his leaving, "finally and for good," he said. Yet I failed to understand why we could not talk and work things out in a "reasonable" way. (I love talking and I realize I am expert at it, and likely to come out the winner; perhaps in choosing my own weapons, I am not being fair.) From my own point of view, his behavior is clearly unreasonable. I searched for reasons.

> *November*
>
> Did we differ in what we wanted? I anticipated that we would discuss, sometimes conflict over, and resolve issues which bothered us over the next year or so. I looked at that anticipated process with some apprehension but with some excitement because I thought we had so much going for us that in the process of being and interacting together we would have an opportunity for growing and for a deeper kind of love. I trusted that there would be space for sharing the lows as well as the highs and that we would both want this and maybe, for you, that was not so.

Deprived of the opportunity to talk, I wrote instead. I inundated him with paper. I guessed at his state of mind, and his reasons for leaving.

> *December*
>
> We have to give up the fantasy that there's some perfect relationship which is never going to hurt. That's hard be-

cause we all want such a relationship but it's never going to be there for any of us, ever. But closeness and intimacy and occasional moments of real highs can be there for those who want to take the chance – and I think you know that.

This attempt at persuasion—education, to my way of thinking—was followed by a reunion, and then a final break. Still, I did not understand *why* (and, of course, part of the problem was that I *expected* to understand why). Yet this time I had been operating on slightly different premises. I had not been so open, I had not shared fully, and I was reexamining this change in my behavior.

March

I decided somewhere along the way, to be very careful in expressing anger to you, and not to talk about anything to you unless I knew whether that was going to be a sensitive area or not. So I stopped telling you my concerns, and I stopped asking questions, and I stopped asking for clarification. And there were many times I simply sat and took in what you were saying — and did not respond because it was very important to me that I be with you and that I feel out first what would be upsetting and what would not.

The result was that I was preoccupied with unsaid things and became distant, saying to myself, there will be time later. All of this reaffirms my belief in openness between intimates and is an example of what I didn't do. I was scared and I withdrew and I argued about peripheral and intellectual issues, and I missed being with you.

I am frightened at the possibility of losing what I believed you and I could have had. I know some of that is still at the fantasy level for me, that it isn't what we had (because I can't lose that) but the potential that I had believed was there for us. I am frightened by the prospect of really being alone, which is still in many ways an unknown for me, and grieving for what might have been.

I had swung from one point of view ("I'll tell you every-thing") to its opposite ("I'll tell you what you want to hear"). A certain naivete lay behind the first assumption, and clearly fear had prompted the second. My first assumptions sprang from the Mature and Reasonable viewpoint, my second from a realization that autonomy often led to aloneness, which I did not want. As I said earlier, the belief in open communication must be accompanied by a belief in autonomy—which, taken to the extreme means being alone. Face to face with being alone, I was quite willing to throw over my beliefs in autonomy—and open communication as well. This was a time of critical reevaluation and aloneness.

This experience of separateness in the world was a good one for me because I came to cherish my relationships more. I did not forsake autonomy entirely, for one must stand up and be able to be alone. Nor did I forsake my belief in open communication entirely, for a relationship will not survive without individuals sharing fully — at times — with each other. But I came to learn that what I thought of as autonomy could sometimes be sacrificed in order to respond to an-other, and that communication could be tempered in order to respect another's space. It is the balancing of autonomy and clarity of communication with an awareness of another that is the key — not autonomy and clarity alone.

The myth of Mature and Reasonable People carries its own pricetag. The new myth, like the Prince Charming one before it, ignores the complexity of human beings. When we ignore the complexity of another (and of ourselves), we may act destructively in a relationship, and that relationship may weaken or die.

As for myself, I began to grope my way toward a new balance. I began to see that full communication requires a shared world view (though it can never be *fully* shared) and that all communication is interpreted from the framework of the other. I had a growing awareness of the different points of view which people bring to relationships, and how these points of view can be destructive in terms of what we most desire (or think we do).

April

A friend of mine says that he wants "totalness" in his relationships. By this he means complete acceptance, constant communication. He believes that if love is real, it will conquer everything else. Yet, he finds that this view doesn't always take him where he wants to be. Nor does it seem to me, at this point, that my own worldview about process, openness and transparency takes me where I want to be. This is so, as my friend pointed out, because some of the things I say would be misinterpreted in an intimate relationship, so that he (my friend) would leave, and he has, at times, left our friendship, but always returned after a while.

I think there must be a meeting point somewhere where the understanding of the other's world precludes acts which are very hurtful and where that sort of understanding also inhibits large-scale misinterpretations of the other. I know I have said and done things, innocuous in my way of thinking, which from your point of view were probably seen as a betrayal of all that we felt for each other. I wonder how one prevents that? Some would say by never having learned to speak at all.

July

... the upshot of the last months is that I have come to temper my belief in transparency and openness with a more traditional emphasis on control and understanding. In recognizing the differences in ways in which communication is interpreted, in recognizing our own difficulties in saying what we mean, in recognizing the importance of what we do not say (and sometimes cannot say), I have emerged in a different place. I am on some new plateau and experience a sense of peace. I hope that you have found this too.

And so, much later, I did indeed revise my thinking. All of the learning from this brief and painful relationship came to fruition in a new and continuing relationship. I make many mistakes, but I am grateful for this new awakening. I am grateful to be entangled neither in the Prince Charming myth nor in the Mature and Reasonable one.

Finally, I have found few rewards as great as living among and caring about others, experiencing all of their complexities as well as my own. To live fully in relationship with others requires a balance of power and love. To have power, a person must be autonomous—to some degree. Out of our strengths, we find the resources to care for others. Love on the other hand, requires that we communicate fully with others, sharing our deepest selves, yet we must also recognize the boundaries of another person: They will not always be ready to receive our disclosures nor will they always interpret them as we would like. Love requires that we respect these idiosyncrasies in others as well as in ourselves. Power gives us the strength to do so.

Thus, power and love still come together in my revision of fulfilling relationships. Yet, I believe I once defined these terms too narrowly. Power as sheer autonomy is so often at the cost of another person—and a relationship. Love as sharing of self without understanding of the other is also a hazard to fulfilling relationships. Yet, power which is a resource for understanding and love which respects the space of the other are still the primary requirements for continuing and fulfilling relationships.

Any mythology, whether Prince Charming or Mature and Reasonable, reduces the complexity of human beings. The heritage of the 1970s was the Mature and Reasonable myth; it rested on a belief in open communication and autonomy. The emphasis on self, and the emphasis on words, was perhaps a tonic for an earlier heritage: caring for others but never telling them anything they do not want to hear. Yet, carried to extremes, defending the principles of communication and autonomy will diminish the possibility of finding those moments of intimacy which sustain us and our relationships.

CHAPTER SIX

LIBERATION: CONFUSIONS AND RESOLUTIONS

In reformulating our outdated concepts of men, women, and relationships, we encounter new permutations of love and power, which are not always understandable nor are they as we would wish them to be. Men and women in transition are seeking new models for living alone and with others yet as they do so, they often appear to be miles away from the goal—the integration of love and power—and miles away from each other as well.

Both sexes, in exploring the capacity to unite love and power, are reacting to the stress of change as each encounters the inner and outer difficulties that bar their paths. Robin Morgan wrote:

> Men have forgotten how to love
> Women have forgotten how not to.
> We must risk unlearning
> What has kept us alive.[1]

Men are opening themselves to the possibilities of love, and women are learning the requirements of power. The process

[1] Robin Morgan, *Monster: Poems by Robin Morgan* (Random House, 1972).

of change is not easy, but we can facilitate the process by recognizing not only our own path of growth, but the differing path of the opposite sex. We must reach out not only to understand ourselves but to understand the other, for men and women face different challenges.

CHANGES IN THE LIVES OF WOMEN

The challenges for women are primarily in the realm of power. Trained to measure their worth in terms of others' affections, women have difficulty going it alone. Yet the use of power requires a recognition of separateness: a willingness to express one's anger at another, to compete and to work toward one's own success. Traditionally, women have deflected their anger with a smile or a sob, competed with men and with each other covertly while discounting their own abilities and, in general, have seen any success as purely a stroke of good luck. Yet, to utilize power well, women must acknowledge their own anger at failure as well as their joy at success; they must give themselves as much credit as they bestow on the goddess of luck.

In the last ten years or so, many women have faced these problems and succeeded in coming to terms with their strength. In the process, women have learned to make friends and allies of each other, and to utilize their own resources as well as those of other women, instead of relying solely on men. In discovering their strength, women have sometimes shouted their newfound power from the rooftops; at other times—scared by their own success—they have retreated to the basements, giving up their power altogether.

Using new capacities is never easy. For women, to be strong means to go against long years of conditioning which have trained her not to win. The development of previously unused capacities is seldom initiated with either grace or balance. What is required, instead, is an extra burst of energy in order to develop these capacities at all. Change is thus an act of courage and women often find this courage in anger.

But after their discovery of anger, strength, and power, many women also found themselves alone. In the early 1960s, many women discovered that what had been called intimacy meant for them a loss of identity. In the 1970s, many women wondered if refinding themselves meant losing their connection with others.

Women have begun to realize, however, that now that they are strong, they can also admit their vulnerabilities; now that they know who they are, they can still spend time in knowing the other. Yet, as women begin again to seek a balance, they recognize—with some consternation—that men too are changing.

CHANGES IN THE LIVES OF MEN

Many changes occurred in men's self-images during the 1970s. Men are still competitive and schooled to rule; their self-esteem still depends on their ability to survive and succeed in the workplace. Yet men are turning inward and questioning themselves, their values, and their needs. They are doing so more than at any other time in the last century. Moreover, they are finding that this process is often less than comfortable.

It is necessary to remember that men have always been enjoined not to think about themselves. Men are supposed to keep their feelings hidden or forget them altogether, and leave the expressive, nurturing, tender sphere to women. Yet the change in our society and in women has released men from the pressure of this injunction. Men have recently been encouraged to examine and to express their feelings, and to be open with others. Thus men are, some for the first time, opening themselves to the messages of their interior selves. This is frightening, since what they are finding inside is a contradictory and complex swarm of instincts, sensations, feelings, and desires.

Yet, at the same time that society encourages men to be more open to their feelings, they are also confronted with women who are more open with their power. Not only have men been shielded by cultural mythology from their inner selves, but they have been protected from confrontation with power in the "lesser sex." No matter what went on in their world, there was always a place to retreat, a succorance that was assured. Now that many women are not automatically providing this reassurance, but rather challenging the male assumption of power and superiority, men are understandably scared not only by what is taking place within themselves, but what is happening in the external world as well.

Scared people often say contradictory things and act in contradictory ways. When men say, as they do today, "I want . . ." followed by "I don't want . . .," "I am . . ." followed by "I'm not . . ." they shatter at every turn the myth of the rational male. Yet men are unable to acknowledge the fear which lies beneath their contradictory behavior, for if they have never learned to handle their feeling and expressive self, they have also never learned to handle fear. By the old fiats of masculinity, men are not supposed to be scared. They not only need time to learn to acknowledge their feelings, but time in which to develop constructive ways with which to handle their fears.

In the meantime, however, men retreat into various familiar cubbyholes to assuage those fears, occasionally re-emerging to give the process of change a second chance. The cubbyholes to which men retreat are all designed to reassure them of their power. A male may react to his own momentary sensitivity by bragging or swaggering a moment later. He may say a word of sympathy about the lives of women and then immediately counter it with a phrase designed to "show a women her place." A man may also strengthen his grip on power by denying his own threatening feelings and anesthetizing himself to his inner experience. Men do this well; they were taught as children how to turn off feelings ("Boys don't cry"), and the pattern is still operative. Such self-anesthesia temporarily reassures frightened men of their power, but at great cost.

RECOGNITION OF FEAR IN THE OPPOSITE SEX

The process of change is, therefore, frightening to both sexes. Men are afraid of losing power; women are afraid of gaining it. Yet women have not been taught to be afraid of their fear as men have, and therefore women have less difficulty recognizing their fears. Although women are afraid of aloneness, power, and success, men are scared of *being scared*; the irrational behavior resulting from this double bind flies in the face of our expectations and beliefs about "rational man." If, however, we can recognize our own and each other's fears, if we can understand that we are both moving toward an integration of love and power, perhaps we can offer each other respect and kindness (though not submission), so that we may not only help ourselves but reach out to help the other.

In order for women to reach out to men with gentleness, however, they must first know themselves very well and know where the lines are drawn. In regaining intimacy, women must not give up selfhood. So, when a twenty-one-year-old woman asks if she should "respect" her live-in boyfriend's desire that she be home at five o'clock every night, and have dinner on the table by five-thirty, even though she works as hard as he does during the day, there are several areas to be explored. Does she know what she wants? Is it important to her and her work that she be later than five on some nights? Does she do all the work around the house for him, including the cooking? The ultimate question is: Does she give up some important sense of self in acceding to his request? Although there are situations in which the answer to the last question is "no," for most twenty-one-year-olds, the answer is "yes"; uncertain about their sense of self, they would not know what they were yielding and what they were preserving.

Yet, many women have come to learn, with time and experience, about the necessary ingredients for selfhood. These may be different for each person. For some women, a sense of self depends on having time to do her work, another may need time to be alone, still another, time to be with friends or children. What are the vital areas that must be preserved? On these issues women need not, as they have in centuries past, compromise; in other areas we may, as before, yield. We must know what is most important to us and what is not, and be willing to respect the wishes of the other, on issues of lesser importance in our experience of self.

For men the issue is different but the task is similar. In order to be open about their feelings, they need not put their business lives on the line, nor give up their necessary sense of power in part of their world. They must know what these things are that matter so much; then they will know what those things are which matter less. Men too can risk trying something new; they too can accommodate the other in ways in which they have not been taught. Men must be open about their feelings more often—not in their business conferences, but in their intimate lives—and they must assess both the internal and external results. They must not anestheticize themselves but rather experience their tenderness and their fears. Yet, as they do this, they must preserve that which is essential to their sense of self. This is perhaps easier for men than for women, for a sense of self is historically possessed by men—and not by women.

For both sexes, the transition to new ways of being is difficult. Self-knowledge is fundamental to the process of change. The ability to distinguish our high-priority needs from our passing desires is equally important. Sometimes we confuse our desires with our important needs; we must work at knowing the difference. Once we know what the vital ingredients of selfhood are, we have come to the point where we can extend our concern to the other. For women coming to a newfound sense of self, and for men who have perhaps been surer of their "self" for longer, it is imperative that we separate the chaff from the wheat and defend only that which is central, allowing the peripheral concerns to be risked in our associations with another.

In conclusion, we can recognize that men and women are still different from each other because they are moving along different developmental pathways. Gone are the days "when men were men and women were women." Yet to come is the point at which we can live fully as complete human beings, unbound by the injunctions attached to our sex. We are, however, on the way. We can help ourselves as well as each other by recognizing our differences as well as our similarities, and come to love and respect the distances we must bridge as well as the closeness of which we are capable. If we can learn to do this with unique individual differences, we can learn to do so for those differences which still remain with us because of our sex-role conditioning.

In order to bring together our views of power and love, to continue the struggle for personal and social integration, we must venture within ourselves. We may then find the resources to venture toward others. The promise of a new integration of love and power lies in this direction.

LIFE CYCLES: PRODUCTIVITY AND INTIMACY

In a previous chapter, I described recent changes in my views on autonomy and openness in relationships. I recognized that in associating power and love with autonomy and openness, I had come to define power and love too narrowly: Power came to represent personal strength and love was the capacity to share oneself with another. In both definitions, the emphasis on self predominates, often at the expense of the relationship. Although I still believe that autonomy and openness are the basic premises of a fulfilling relationship, they must be balanced with a concern for the other and for the relationship.

In this chapter, I examine the concept of equality between partners. Equality is defined specifically as the absence of the inequities which exist between men and women *because they are men and women.* As I examine and revise my views of equality in relationships, I return again to questions of autonomy and openness. The setting is, however, different, instead of describing male-female relationships in general, I am focusing on the dual-career marriage over the life cycle. I ask how dual-career marriages survive the stresses and strains that impinge on two adults with two careers and at least one child. The conclusion I come to is that our emphasis on total equality in a relationship is sometimes counterproductive in this situation, and as a result of this emphasis we may argue ourselves right out of the intimacy we seek. I have not given up the concept of equality, but rather broadened and expanded the definition which guides my own experience.

THE MYTH OF PERFECT EQUALITY IN MODERN MARRIAGE

In my own life, I have discovered remnants of my feminine conditioning that I want to keep rather than throw out. Yet, I retain my strong belief in the importance of intimacy, recognizing that intimacy can be attained only between two relatively equal, open human beings. How can such an apparent retreat from feminism, from humanism, and from equality be explained? The fact that, in our world, men still want to be powerful and women still want to be loved *is not necessarily incompatible* with the movement toward a more human universe in which men and women both work and love.

The recent cultural emphasis on intimacy has led psychologists to propound an equalitarian view of interpersonal relationships, in which two full human beings join together—open, sharing, and equal. In this ideal vision of intimate relationships, gender roles drop away, power is never an issue, and each fully accepts the other. Many of us do experience the delights of such intimacy—most often in periods of ease, relaxation, and well-being. These are the best of times. But these are not the times when the children are sick, the paycheck has gotten sidetracked, or company is coming and the house is a mess. Nor are these the times when publishing deadlines have passed, grant proposals have been denied, and job tenure is in question. Yet, it is this underside of both home and work life which occupies so much of our time. In such times, two warm, loving, open human beings can temporarily become angry enemies; the value of openness and equality in such times depreciates markedly. Under the guise of "openness" human beings can say some devastating things to each other. The spirit of give-and-take may turn quickly into a philosophy of an eye for an eye. At such times traditional sex roles become an asset and not a liability. They provide a means for soothing the irritated soul by familiar patterns, and the familiarity may provide a respite from defensiveness and alienation. To explain this notion further, I must speak first about the change from old cultural norms to new ones, and the conflict that is created by living in between the two.

The notion of openness and equality in interpersonal relationships are accepted by many more people today; blatant sexism is out and equality is in. Feminism and the human potential movement have helped to create a personal growth ethic which gives equal opportunity to both sexes. Part of this ethic is the belief, that, if we live right, we may be able to do it all: to have creative work and also enjoy excellent human relationships with equal human beings both personally and professionally. We not only believe this—particularly women—but we have tried hard to make it work. Yet these new norms contradict our personal and cultural heritage.

Those of us who grew up in less "liberated" times may have buried within us an entirely different view of life from the one espoused by equalitarian feminists and humanists. We carry within us two sets of norms, the new ones (located in the head region), and the old ones (located in our gut). When all is going well in a world directed by our heads (and our hearts), we treat other people as valuable human beings and we respect the notion of equality. Yet, in times of stress, which occur fairly regularly, more basic instincts take over. At such times we retreat to our traditional picture of the world: Men want to know that they are in control and women want to know that they are loved. Then, reassured by familiarity, we are able to move forward again.

Conflicting norms, of course, lead to anxiety and inner tension. As long as we carry such conflicting norms within us, we need to acknowledge both sets of values, contradictory though they may be. If we refuse to acknowledge both sets of values, we may be pushed unconsciously by the one that we have neglected.

THE RECOGNITION OF TRADITIONAL SEX ROLES

The application of this principle in a two-career family involves numerous recognitions of male "superiority," which I used to find unacceptable. In practice, this means that the male does not have the nominal head-of-household title, that he receives appreciation for his "household help," and that both parties acquiesce in sex-role divisions of labor when efficiency and tolerance threshholds make this a reasonable course. This kind of behavior provides a nonthreatening atmosphere in which the new part of ourselves can grow and appreciate the old part. We all need to recognize the ambivalence and complexity of the current transitional period and allow ourselves to live the complexity fully. Occasionally, this means acknowledging the symbolic importance of traditional sex-role behavior.

I do not advocate a return to traditional norms, in which men's and women's roles are very distinct from each other, and the partners seldom share the high point of communion which does happen periodically in the best of relationships. However, neither do I advocate the pursuit of equality at all times. I am suggesting that we strive for a delicate balance in which each part of ourselves, the old and the new, is acknowledged, and the symbolic ritual of traditional sex-role behavior paves the way for a fuller acceptance of human beings in both work and love. To achieve the balance where one can do both creative work and share with another person, we must recognize both the internal and the external realities with which we live. If this appears to be an acquiescence to old norms of male dominance, in some ways, perhaps it is. Yet a recognition of our existing reality provides a better starting point for making behavioral decisions than a utopia which is not yet here, and whose advent is becoming somewhat suspect.

After concluding that intimacy might, in fact, require occasional recognition of traditional sex-role behavior, I spoke with numerous couples who declared that this was not their experience: Their own behavior did not demonstrate any obeisance to sex-role norms in either task allocation or personal expression. However, these couples were, at this time, each engaged in highly productive activity which furthered their careers and claimed the majority of their attention. Placing a priority on productivity is more likely to lead to an overtly equalitarian marriage than placing a priority on intimacy. In the life cycle of both individuals and relationships, different values may predominate at different points in time.

THE EVOLUTION OF MARRIAGE: PAST AND PRESENT

Historically, the marriage relationship has been characterized by an emphasis on productivity: Men (and sometimes women) worked to ensure the survival of the family unit; women bore and raised children to ensure the perpetuation of the family. Much of a couple's adult years were spent in these tasks which were generally viewed as essential to survival. The necessity for such productivity, both at work and at home, overrode other considerations and, in many ways, stabilized the marriage. Relationships, centered on productivity, were noted for their longevity. Others have pointed out that these marriages survived because the bonds were economic: A woman was dependent economically on her husband. Because of changes in recent decades—shorter work hours, smaller families, and the influx of women into the labor market—these are no longer the only considerations.

With economic survival no longer the primary issue, many marriages today, especially dual-career couples, place much more emphasis on emotional satisfaction. This has led to a higher divorce rate, an increase in remarriage, and an exploration of nontraditional forms of relationship. Marriages based primarily on emotional considerations are more likely to terminate as individuals grow, change, and seek new levels of fulfillment in their lives. Though intimacy and productivity may go together in the best of times, the relationship geared to intimacy is very different from the relationship geared to productivity: The goals, behavior, and values acknowledged all differ in the two orientations.

INTIMACY AND PRODUCTIVITY IN RELATIONSHIPS

In the productive relationship, the adaptation to the "real world," is the primary consideration. In many ways, this orientation requires a predominance of the head over the heart, and instinctive feelings are subordinated to the current needs of productive activity. Emotional dissatisfaction is compensated for by the achievement of productive goals.

The power in such relationships is generally allocated in accord with productivity—in most relationships the male contributes more economically and thus he has the edge in power. However, in some dual-career marriages, both the man and woman contribute equally and the result may be a genuinely equalitarian relationship.

In the intimate relationship emotional satisfaction is primary: the "whole person," including both old and new sets of norms, demands recognition. Both the old and the new, and the contradiction that they pose, become part of the relationship. Since genuine intimacy occurs only among equals, both persons must recognize the value and worth of the other; neither is consistently the child to the other's adult, and neither is subservient and selfless. Though the relationship is, at the best of times, equal, such equality is nonetheless accompanied by a recognition of traditional masculine and traditional feminine needs. Both the male need to control and the female need to be cherished is acknowledged, even though both men and women want to be cherished and want to control at times. The self-esteem of each sex, however, is tied more to one than the other.

It is important to stress at this point that the symbolic recognition of occasional male dominance is accompanied by a recognition of equality in many spheres. Our concern here is with couples who *both* have an investment in their careers as well as their relationship, and especially couples who have children, the continual pressure to meet three sets of demands (children, career, and marriage), necessitates the juggling of responsibilities in order to meet a demanding time schedule.

There may be, however, a time sequence in the life cycle of a relationship in which priorities on productivity and intimacy appear at different times. In the first seven to ten years of a career, for example (and, often, a marriage), one's later career success is determined. For those who have set their sights high, this may induce a sense of crisis in the early professional years. If this is so, and an emphasis on productivity in a relationship is related to one's career aspirations, then couples emerging from this period may later shift their priorities, when other needs may become more pressing. For example, at the end of a productivity cycle, the search for emotional satisfaction may supersede the requirements of productivity. Economic pressures may be lessened and new, as yet unclarified, priorities may demand recognition. At this point, when the immediate demands of a professional career have eased, many individuals engage in a renewed search for intimacy in their lives.

A priority on either productivity or intimacy continues to alternate throughout the life cycle; at each level one may find a higher form of integration of the two. As one grows and matures, the cycles of power and love (for that is indeed what productivity and intimacy reflect) alternate with each other more quickly, and each alternation signals yet a new integration, in which neither power nor love becomes completely subservient to the other.

PART III

WOMEN AND MEN
AT WORK

CHAPTER EIGHT

OUTSIDERS ON THE INSIDE: WOMEN AND ORGANIZATIONS

The organizational world is structured according to the rules of power. It is hierarchical, categorical, and supposedly rational. It has been the province of men for a long time and is structured according to male assumptions. Women entering this world bring with them another set of assumptions. Many of their expectations have been formulated by the world of love, the emphasis of which is equality and emotionality. In entering this world, women are outsiders who face three distinct challenges. In this chapter we examine the challenges faced by women as they enter the work world and become outsiders on the inside, as well as the possibilities for change inherent in those challenges.

THE CHALLENGES FACED BY THE OUTSIDER

The first challenge confronting the outsider is definition of self and other. Upon entrance into a new group, outsiders—by their very presence—raise questions about what the German sociologist Alfred Schutz calls "thinking as usual."[1]

---

[1] Alfred Schutz, "The Stranger," in *The Psychology of Society*, R. Sennett, ed. (New York: Vintage, 1977), pp. 141–49.

Schutz states that for any given group, group life "takes on . . . sufficient coherence, clarity, and consistency to give anybody a reasonable chance of understanding or being understood." Certain assumptions that the group makes about human behavior are taken for granted; this constitutes "thinking as usual." These assumptions are not examined though they often encompass logical inconsistencies and outdated customs which no insider chooses to question. Yet outsiders, entering with a different set of assumptions, are shocked that the "thinking as usual" of the in-group is not the same as that of the group from which they came. Their very presence thus calls into question all accepted norms, both those of the outsiders and those on the inside.

The result, says Schutz, is that the stranger needs to define the situation with explicit knowledge of its elements. Outsiders need to ask *why* as well as *how*. Consequently, they bring into question for themselves and for others all customary ways of behavior. This questioning leads to a greater objectivity on the part of outsiders. They are the ones who can—and who must—ask why. Thus outsiders are forced into an analysis of themselves and of the system they have entered and, from their vantage point, they can see more objectively both self and others.

Secondly, outsiders are called upon to seek a new definition of themselves within the context of the unfamiliar group. British philosopher Colin Wilson writes about outsiders throughout intellectual history, illustrating the anguish and torment experienced by the romantics—philosophers, poets and artists—who found themselves outside the scientific, rational mainstream of Western society. He finds that for most of these individuals the position of outsider poses the difficult question of self-redefinition:

> . . . the Outsider always aims at ceasing to be an Outsider. . . . The question that then presents itself is: Toward what? If he doesn't want to be an Outsider, and he

> doesn't want to be an ordinary well-adjusted social being, what the devil *does* he want to become?[2]

In terms of the in-group, outsiders are persons without precedent and without history. Not wishing to remain outside, and not able to be fully inside, they must find some new integration of outside and inside that will provide constructive self-definition.

The third challenge lies in *how* the outsider approaches the task of self-redefinition. The outsider may seek a personal, idiosyncratic solution which leaves untouched the intrinsic problems of outsider status ("I will attach myself to a powerful other and work under her patronage"; "I will not rock the boat, but I will save enough money to leave this group as soon as possible"). Or the outsider may choose to address this problem by translating her problem into larger terms ("I will through law, art, or whatever my personal medium, act to illustrate and possibly better the situation of all in my position."). By addressing the problem in what might be termed an existential context, the impact of the outsider's personal resolution will affect others both within and without the system.

Psychologists Charles Hampton-Turner[3] and Liam Hudson[4] point out that innovations have always been introduced by those who are initially peripheral to the system. The particular position of the outsider, which may involve personal anguish, encourages a marriage of objectivity with strong subjective motivation: A new integration may thus emerge from the clash of the inside and the outside. In so doing, the outsider reshapes her personal world as well as the world of others.

[2] Colin Wilson, *The Outsider* (New York: Delta, 1956).
[3] Charles Hampton-Turner, *Radical Man* (Garden City: N.Y.: Anchor/Doubleday, 1977).
[4] Liam Hudson, *Human Beings* (Garden City, N.Y.: Doubleday, 1975).

To summarize, outsiders have a perspective from which they are required to assess themselves and assess the system; they are required as well to find a new definition of self in terms of the group which they are joining; and, depending on the depth and breadth of this new self-definition, they will affect the system, and bridge some of the differences between the inside and outside.

THE PUBLIC SPHERE: A MASCULINE IMPERATIVE

The position of outsider well describes the situation of women in the male-dominated organizational world. The world of organizations is the major expression of the public sphere in American life—and it has always been controlled by males. Institutions have been originated, designed, and analyzed by men. Ideologies have been created and perpetuated by men. New forms of government have been created by men; the same sex has demolished forms of government no longer thought functional. Underlying all of these activities lies the assumption that what is good for men is good for people since, in fact, one rarely questioned the predominance and pervasiveness of the male orientation. "By the people, for the people, and of the people" really means "By men, for men, and of men." The phrase reflects the male's perennial confusion of himself with people in general.

The public sphere, according to many psychologists and sociologists, is dominated by values of independence, rationality, and self-reliance; these are the legitimized values of American culture. The values embodied by our public institutions—political, economic, social, or educational—are those values which coincide with the usual definitions of masculinity. The private sphere, on the other hand, encourages dependence, emotionality, nurturance, and sometimes aesthetic pursuits. As important and human as these values are, they are nonetheless peripheral to the mainstream of American culture. These are the illegitimate values which throughout our history have been assigned to "the Other," to use Simone de Beauvoir's term, and have been relegated to women.[5] In talking about the private sphere, it is then no surprise that those values coincide with standard definitions of femininity.

The world of organizations—social, political or economic— is thus identified with the public sphere and with the behavior of men. Descriptions of business organizations by organizational psychologists reflect this male orientation. For example, organizations have been described in terms of progress, efficiency, rationality, achievement, and success. Organizations stress technical competence and rational mediation.[6] Organizational bureaucracy, as defined by Max Weber, is modeled after the rational man who can keep his personal affairs to himself. The result, in terms of organizational structure, has been the institutionalization of a division of labor; a hierarchy of authority; a system of rules and procedures which deals with categories, not individuals; and the development and enforcement of norms of impersonality which govern the organization. Robert Merton says that it is expected, therefore, that men in organizations be methodical, prudent, disciplined, reliable, conforming, and impersonal.

Such personality configurations are demanded not only by organizations but throughout the public sphere. They are based on the characteristics associated with the use of overt power in our society in which distance between others is

[5] Simone de Beauvoir, *The Second Sex* (New York: Knopf, 1953).

[6] W. Bennis, *Changing Organizations* (New York: McGraw-Hill, 1966); F. W. Neff, *Managing Change in Organizations* (Ann Arbor: Foundation for Research on Human Behavior, 1961); R. K. Merton, "Bureaucratic Structure and Personality," *Social Forces*, 23 (1945), pp. 404–15.

a prerequisite for influence over them. Men have been trained to live by the concepts of rationality and power. They have learned to live with hierarchies, with categories, with impersonality, and with separateness. Women, however, enter the organization from the private sphere, trailing mythological associations with emotions, personal concerns, and dependence. Women socialized into the world of love, thus enter organizations with a set of beliefs about the world which differ from those of men. Thus, in the work force, women are outsiders. They do not "fit" and they call into question all the beliefs about the inside and the outside which have been taken for granted for centuries.

THE ENTRANCE OF WOMEN INTO THE PUBLIC SPHERE

It is clear then that women will not be warmly welcomed into a world to which, historically, they do not belong. Their very presence is a threat to the assumptions underlying these organizations. Their presence in the work force is also, because of the dissonant perceptions of others, a challenge to their own sense of self. The difficulties which women incur because of their outsider status will be examined in turn.

Women, on entering the work force, must first deal with the shock of recognizing the distorted perceptions which others hold of them. In the organizational world, women are distinctly different from those who have preceded them; they do not match any of the previously developed concepts of how workers should behave. There is no category in the minds of insiders which can encompass the full perception of another's individuality when that individuality is in female form. Women are thus viewed through the old stereotyped categories and are seen as bitch, witch, pet, or doll. Moreover, if women's behavior eludes these categories, the women are perceived as unknowable and therefore threatening. The insider's reaction to the threat is to psychologically wipe the threat from view. A woman at work is an anomaly and an exception, obviously a mistake, and hence is best tolerated by lack of recognition. The invisibility of outsiders in general thus is extended to working women and prevents them from the full exercise of their talents.

Women entering the workplace, therefore, often encounter a cultural shock: their accustomed visibility when they are in their place (the private sphere) is suddenly replaced by the invisibility of their presence now that they are out of place (in the public sphere). The lack of recognition by others leads to a devaluing of their own competence. The lack of confirmation by others leads to questioning of one's intrinsic self-worth. This is the lot of all outsiders.

As they are experiencing the clash between the female and male realities (and the resulting lack of confirmation extended by the more powerful male), women also encounter another area of cultural shock, as does a newcomer to any organization. John Van Maanen describes the experience this way:

> Like laymen visiting the laboratory of a nuclear physicist, newcomers to an organization are blind to many of the defining characteristics of their immediate setting. Novices must learn, therefore, how and what to see and hear.[7]

Yet, at this point, women's and men's similarity as newcomers ends. For after being stunned by a new set of expectations, men are picked up, dusted off, and set on the appropriate track by those who have gone before them. Men are taught their work while on the job: They are given challenging tasks, evaluated both critically and positively, and

[7] John Van Maanen, "Experiencing Organizations: Notes on the Meaning of Careers and Socialization," in *Organizational Careers: Some New Perspectives,* John Van Maanen, ed. (New York: John Wiley, 1977).

given the assistance and protection of more established males.

Women, on the other hand, are left standing at the door-step, still stunned by the experience of entering an alien culture. They are not picked up and set on the track, for those who have gone before do not recognize any redeeming similarities in newcomers who happen to be women, nor do they foresee future success for the newcomer, for there are no precedents against which women can be measured. Consequently, women are often not subjected to the disciplines of their profession; instead they are victimized by lowered expectations and lowered rewards and, as Cynthia Fuchs Epstein points out, they are "subject to the subtle cooling-out process that men experience as individuals."[8]

In the current age of superficial liberation, however, this cooling-out process may be well-disguised. Overlooking her errors, emphasizing her femininity by compliments and sexual overtures, not demanding too much, and not taking her work seriously, are all ways in which women are not treated to the full rigor of on-the-job socialization.

Another challenge facing women is to define their own self-concept. In the face of all of these difficulties and skewed perceptions, who is it that women want to be? Do they want to be like men? Do they want to behave like traditional women? Or have they the strength to carve out a path somewhere in between?

THE CHALLENGE FOR WOMEN: CARVING OUT A MIDDLE GROUND

It was noted earlier that, in general, men are trained to the realm of power and women to the realm of love. In many ways, men and traditional women represent the separation

[8] Cynthia Fuchs Epstein, "Bring Women In: Rewards, Punishments and the Structure of Achievement," in *Women and Success*, R. Kundsen, ed. (New York: Morrow, 1974).

of the realms of power and love. However, working women cannot afford this traditional separation; if they wish to remain in the workforce they must learn the game of power. If they wish to retain their humanity, however, they must not leave behind the realm of love. They must demonstrate both task competence and interpersonal skill, bringing together the two spheres of love and power, and, in the process, carving out a new model of how people can be.

Asking this of working women, however, is asking more of them than we ask of either men or traditional women. Our culture provides models of behavior that preclude the hard struggle for personal integration which, as psychologists have reminded us since the time of Freud, requires both the capacity to work creatively and to care for others; in other words, the integration of power and love. For working women, this integration is not a luxury, but a necessity, and the new integration which they achieve may provide models for others who enter the workplace, so that a new way of living and working can come into being.

WORKING WOMEN: A DISTORTED PICTURE

Much of the research on women and work demonstrates that women are not perceived in the same terms as men in organizations. Numerous studies show that women are believed to be less suited for supervisory, managerial, or executive positions.[9] A recent national survey, in fact, finds

[9] G. W. Bowman, N. B. Worthy, and S. A. Greyser, "Are Women Executives People?," *Harvard Business Review*, 43 (1965), pp. 14–16; E. A. Cecil, R. J. Paul, and R. A. Olins, "Perceived Importance of Selected Variables Used to Evaluate Male and Female Job Applicants," *Personnel Psychology*, 26 (1973), pp. 397–404; S. Cohen and K. Bunker, "Subtle Effects of Sex-Role Stereotypes on Recruiters' Hiring Decisions," *Journal of Applied Psychology*, 60 (1975), pp. 566–72; R. L. Dipboye, H. L. Fromkin, and K. Wilback, "Relative Importance of Applicant Sex, Attractiveness, and Scholastic Standing in Evaluation of Job Applicant Resumes," *Journal of Applied Psychology*, 60 (1975), pp. 39–43.

that the old stereotypes of working women are still with us. In a survey of nearly 900 managers and administrators, men were perceived as different from women and men were perceived as *better*. The specific list of traits and behavior patterns by which men were differentiated from women is strong confirmation of the outside status of women.[10]

Rosen and Jerdee in this study found, for example, that men were perceived as better at understanding the "big picture" of the organization, approaching problems rationally, getting people to work together, understanding financial matters, sizing up situations accurately, and administering and holding leadership positions. In addition, they were said to stand up under fire, keep cool in emergencies, be independent, self-sufficient, and aggressive. Finally, they were seen as having math aptitude, the capacity to set long range goals, and the desire to succeed. Women, on the other hand, were seen as better at doing clerical tasks and detail work. Women were also perceived as crying easily, being sensitive to criticism, being timid, jealous, and too emotional. Finally, women were perceived as not wanting to get ahead, often absent, and likely to quit.

These are the current stereotypes which still shape the perceptions of women in the workforce. Although we know that these stereotypes are breaking down in some professions most women will still find their self-image set askew by the distorted perceptions which they encounter upon entrance into the workplace.[11] We know that the behavior of men and women on the job is not all that different. Behavior in successful executives, whether they are male or female, is rated similarly in effectiveness by their peers and subordinates. Other studies show that women are not absent more often than men, and do not quit more frequently when

[10] B. Rosen and T. Jerdee, "Perceived Sex Differences in Managerially Relevant Characteristics," *Sex Roles*, 4 (1978), pp. 837–44.

[11] Epstein, 1974.

status and job seniority are matched.[12] However, to the extent that they exist, many of the differences in male and female behavior at work can be accounted for by the fact that generally men have the better jobs. Most women in the workforce are in job situations for which they are overqualified and underpaid, and as Rosabeth Kanter makes clear in *Men and Women of the Corporation*, the foot-dragging behavior of those who perceive small promise in their jobs is somewhat similar in both men and women.[13] The figures on working women testify to this situation: Men have better jobs and are paid more; women have less challenging jobs and are paid less. In contrast to the relatively equal levels of education in the two sexes, the job differentials stand out as alarming indications of discrimination.

For example, in 1977, 42.1% of the United States workforce was composed of women; 56% of women at least sixteen years of age worked all or part of the year. Yet of this number, 80% of the women are in clerical, sales, service, factory, or plant jobs. Moreover, in 1977 full-time women workers had a median income of $6,256 less than men. On the average, full-time working women earned 59 cents for each dollar earned by working men.[14] In higher level jobs, even though women are in 30% to 50% of the entry level management positions today, only 5% of middle managers and only a minuscule proportion of top managers are women.[15] Clearly, women—whose formal education is similar to men—have a dissimilar experience of the work world.

[12] Margaret Mead and Frances Kaplan, eds., *American Women: The Report of the Presidents' Commission on the Status of Women* (New York: Charles Scribners Sons, 1965).

[13] Rosabeth Kanter, *Men and Women in the Corporation* (New York: Basic Books, 1977).

[14] Bureau of Labor Statistics, 1978.

[15] M. Hennig and A. Jardim, "Women in Management" (presentation at the Annual Meeting of the Women in Personnel and Communications Association, Detroit, April, 1978).

They find themselves in jobs which do not challenge or excite them, nor promise potential development of their talents. The distribution of jobs between the sexes, indeed, represents the distorted stereotypical views we have of men and women.

This same sense of distortion influences the evaluation of women's work in organizations. Though behavior of men and women in equal positions is often not very different, men and women are evaluated differently. Women are generally seen as performing less well than men even when performance is similar. On occasion they are evaluated more highly than men because one is so surprised to see them working at all. Yet, whether they are rated better or worse than men, they are evaluated on more global characteristics than their male peers. Women are not evaluated just for their competence, but for their looks, their personalities, and their ability to navigate through the subtle discrimination with which they contend.[16]

INTEGRATION OF POWER AND LOVE IN THE WORK WORLD

Yet, some women are succeeeding in the workforce and doing so remarkably well. These successful women seem to have come to their own unique balance of task competence and interpersonal skills. They have been able, as Judith Bardwick notes of her own behavior, to be both evaluative and warmly personal with their employees.[17] They are able, in fact, to integrate the dimensions of power and love.

[16] F. Fuller and M. Batchelder, "Opportunities for Women at the Administrative Level," *Harvard Business Review* (January-February, 1953), pp. 111–28; N. Wikler, "Sexism in the Classroom" (paper presented at the American Sociology Association Annual Meeting, New York, September, 1976).

[17] Judith Bardwick, "An Administrator's Viewpoint: The Interaction of Sex and Power," in *Outsiders on the Inside: Women and Organizations*, Barbara Forisha and Barbara Goldman, eds., (Englewood Cliffs, N.J.: Prentice-Hall, 1981).

This is, however, a monumental task and one which we cannot expect all, or even most, women to accomplish. The acceptance of many women in the workforce will, therefore, most likely await a change in structural factors. The women who succeed are now blazing the path for those who will follow and establishing patterns of behavior which may eventually result in a new structural integration of the inside and outside. Some of the indications of these changes are seen in the new work relationships being formed by women with men, and women with each other.

As mentioned earlier, newcomers to an organization go through a period of informal on-the-job training that acculturates them to the organization. Often this learning period occurs because the newcomer has been selected by a more established person and the two develop a pupil-mentor relationship. This process does not occur naturally for women who are perceived as different. However, successful women have found ways to receive support from their male peers and superiors—either through the traditional mentor relationship or by piecing together a complete "mentor" from the partial support offered by several men.[18] Many of these women are developing male-female professional relationships which break down previous stereotypes and paves the way for women later to develop similar relationships.

In addition, as more women enter the workforce they are beginning to do this for each other to a greater extent than has occurred before. For many women, the support of other women in similar situations is absolutely necessary. Thus, to the extent that women form networks, sponsorships, and superior-subordinate relationships with each other, they provide professional and personal support which stands against the pressures of subtle discrimination. They

---

[18] M. Rowe, "Mentors in Organizations" (presentation at seminar series, "Women and Men in the Academic World," Dearborn, MI., November, 1978).

also give to other women the personal confirmation accompanying clear perception of each other, thus making easier the route to personal integration demanded of women at work.

It is clear from the work of Rosabeth Kanter, as well as others, that a greater number of women in the workforce will not only improve the psychological, but also the structural, situation of women. Outsiders are outsiders partially because they are vastly outnumbered. As increasing numbers of women enter the workforce, and learn both to use their power and to help each other, there is bound to be a change brought about by their presence. The change which they encourage promises to be in the direction that organizational theorists have been saying would be beneficial for the insider as well as the outsider. Women will bring a new measure of interpersonal skill, united with competence, into the work world. It may be that this combination of love and power within every individual is becoming a mandate for successful living in a time of rapid social change.

In beginning this change, women are bringing the sphere of the private world to the door of the public domain, and on entering they unite the mythological private and public spheres. It may be that ultimately, like all outsiders, women who are successful on the male-dominated "inside" will change the shape and nature of organizations so that we will all learn to work in a humane and productive climate. This is the promise of the new integration which women as outsiders may wrest from the clash between outside and inside realities.

CHAPTER NINE

PYRAMIDS AND CIRCLES: IMAGES OF POWER

From the contextual frameworks in which men and women grow up, we shape our views of power in the workplace. Men grow up with images of pyramids always at the periphery of their vision. They perceive, however dimly, that the external world is structured with many at the bottom and a few at the top, and that a hierarchical order is pervasive. They know, too, that someday they must enter that world, or drop out of society altogether. Women, on the other hand, grow up with images of relationships and systems as expanding circles. There is no pyramid in their peripheral vision inexorably claiming their future potential; there is no hierarchical structure bred into their view of life. Rather, the horizon is flat, and individuals oscillate closer to or farther from center in expanding waves of community in which each is equal to the other. Men thus grow up with an up-down dimension engrained in their mind; women's thought has, primarily, an in-out dimension, a measure of her centrality in the world.

This is another way of saying that men are socialized into a world of power and women are socialized into a world of love. Women learn early that love is central to their lives and they fear that moving up and down a hierarchical structure will interfere with their ability to love and be loved. Men, in contrast, have learned that achievement is central to their identity and they fear that allowing themselves the luxury of equality in the circular world of love will interfere with their ability to succeed. The thinking of each sex is therefore formulated according to different expectations derived from either the world of love or power.

PROBLEMS WITH THE DEMOCRATIC PROCESS

What does this mean in terms of the behavior of men and women in the work place? It means that the behavior of many working women is out of step with the assumptions which govern most organizational behavior. Our formal institutions are based on a model created by men. This model assumes the necessity of a hierarchical structure. It assumes that the world is structured in a pyramidal form. Yet women—behaving as if the world were circular and flat— often demonstrate behavior which appears unusual and odd. Often this behavior is termed incompetent, since competence is the chief measuring stick of the organizational world. I tend periodically to share this view about the behavior of other women and some men. Let me give you a few examples.[1]

Recently, I was asked to be a member of a committee, composed primarily of graduate student women, who were

[1] In each of these examples, I am describing behavior that I perceived as detrimental to the goals of the group. However, there are many instances in each group in which matters were handled quite differently and very effectively. In all cases, the individuals involved eventually met their objectives. There are many instances of positive behavior I could cite drawn from the same groups of people. It is the negative instances taken together, however, that point the way to common threads in female organizational behavior. Along with other psychologists, I believe we often learn about how people think and what their expectations are when things are going poorly more than when they are going well.

revising a major course to meet the standards of the college curriculum committee. I initially joined the committee because of misleading communication between myself and a senior faculty woman. She had asked me to consider teaching a course in her department for the next year and said some graduate students would call to discuss this with me. In the phone call I was asked to attend the committee meetings. I did not clarify the purpose of these meetings, and consequently, partly due to my negligence, wound up sitting through meetings whose purpose was not entirely clear to me.

I believe now that what occurred was the faculty woman assumed that the major problem in approving the new course was in appointing an established instructor who could both design and teach the course. This was, however, a department in which graduate students were heavily involved in both designing curriculum and teaching courses. The graduate students, on the other hand, assumed that they would design the course and then choose the instructor. Consequently, I was to be a member of the committee which would restructure the curriculum—and possibly, in their eyes, a potential instructor.

I doubt that either the faculty or the students had communicated clearly with each other. Further, I did not rectify this situation, so I found myself in a series of meetings, anticipating that instructor selection was the major focus. As the nature of the meetings became more clear to me I asked to be excused, pleading more pressing commitments. Another senior faculty woman suggested that I continue to attend the meetings (which, she, herself, did not attend). After one more meeting, I made my apologies and took care of my other commitments.

What was going on at these meetings? There was little that had any direct bearing on curriculum development. There was much that was interesting, however, in terms of group process. Although I frequently participate in committee meetings of all sorts, I found myself in a foreign world. The meetings were not led by the persons who had the most knowledge on the subject nor the greatest leadership ability. Long periods of time were spent discussing subjects only tangentially relevant to what was purported to be the main topic. There was an agenda which was not followed. There was a concerted effort to let each person talk as much as she wished to—that is, everyone but the few faculty women in attendance. At the conclusion of each meeting, a new session was called for with some eagerness and excitement—because so little had been accomplished.

I am not suggesting that most committees operate any more effectively than this one. Yet the *manner* of ineffectiveness was quite different. Two remarks made during the course of these several weeks were illuminating. One of the senior faculty women privately told me when I was preparing to make my excuses that it was important for me to attend because *the graduate women had difficulty interacting with faculty women* and this would be a learning experience for them.

The second remark was made by A., a graduate woman on the committee whose course was well-received by students and curriculum committees alike. She periodically introjected some temporary organizational structure into early meetings before the discussion once again veered offcourse. Someone commented that perhaps A.'s course might become a model for the one under discussion. A. said that was not possible since in creating her course she—in contrast to those present—*had not been bothered by the notion of democratic process.*

Was this a democratic process I was observing or a permutation of it? What occurred at these meetings certainly reflected one interpretation of the democratic process. It was assumed that all individuals, regardless of status, experience, or skill, were to be treated as equals. This assumption created the students' difficulty in interacting with faculty women who often had more experience, knowledge, and skill than their younger counterparts. In addition, their notion of democratic process prevented construction of a viable course outline.

In many settings, the assumptions of equality facilitate a sense of self-confirmation in participants as well as an exchange of information. In this particular setting, however, other priorities intruded. First, the committee had a task and a deadline which had been imposed by a higher body in the large university system. Second, it was critical to the survival of this program that the deadline be met on time and to the satisfaction of that higher body. Third, in order to accomplish its task, this committee required the assistance of individuals who had more experience than they and whose time was in somewhat short supply. The necessity of meeting responsibilities assigned by a larger system within a given time framework made their assumptions about equality inappropriate. To an ordinary observer from the organizational world, these women would appear incompetent. However, their competence per se was really not in question. Rather, the assumptions upon which they were operating were inappropriate to their function.[2]

Soon after this, I consulted with another women's group. In outward appearance, they were totally different from the graduate women. The graduate students had worn jeans and flannel shirts, their hair pulled back in rubber bands or cut quite short, and no make-up. In contrast, the women in the second group were dressed in tailored suits and soft blouses, had neatly coiffed hair and meticulously applied make-up in subtle shades. This second group of women met not in a barren university room, but in down-

[2] The graduate women did succeed in developing a coherent, comprehensive course outline; yet this accomplishment occurred because one faculty woman (not myself) and one graduate woman met separately from the rest of the committee for several hours and met the requirements of the task.

town restaurants and in plush apartments high above the city. They were mid-level managers for a large corporation.

Initially, these women from different divisions of the corporation had met as a support group to share problems and exchange information. Within this framework, they had treated each other as equals, equivalent in status, function, and experience; they had formed a bond which had sustained them through the course of a year. When I met them, the purposes of the group were changing; the women were faced with the task of initiating a large, corporation-wide network of women managers. They were having difficulty making this transition from support to task-accomplishment.

Faced with a deadline for a corporate presentation, the group split into factions. Two or three women would band together and oppose suggestions put forth by the other side. This opposition was never manifested in confrontation but rather in delays, extended discussions, and subtle sabotage of previously agreed-upon plans. The chief weapon in the arsenal of the foot-draggers was "the democratic process." Everybody had to be consulted, every opinion had to be heard, and everybody had to agree. Finally, one assertive woman—impatient with the indecision—undertook to make most of the decisions and do most of the work. She arranged the corporate presentation splendidly and with great success. In the process, however, she incurred the resentment of the rest of the group. At the next meeting in a split vote the group elected another woman president who, it was hoped, would not so distinguish herself from the other group members.[3]

[3] These managers have also succeeded since in becoming a task-oriented group. The transition was difficult, and they have lost some members and gained others. Further, their new president may indeed decide to "rock the boat." She has the added advantage in this position of having high status on the outside—which is good for the group politically. Furthermore, if she does not decide to move the group toward action, she will become the figurehead while others do the job for her.

STATUS DIFFERENCES AMONG WOMEN COWORKERS

These experiences are both recent, although my interest in women's groups is of long standing. However, it has taken a number of years for me to ask if women's groups, or women working together at high levels, have any particular problems which are less common in the ranks of men. A year or so ago, I gave this some thought in terms of individual women working together. Several brief incidents occurred at once which led me to seek a common denominator. At the time, one woman faculty member commented over lunch that she had a fair amount of difficulty in working with graduate assistants who were women. She said there was an antagonism in the relationship which she did not understand. At the same time, another woman colleague of mine was temporarily sabotaged in a major research project by a female research assistant who concocted innumerable reasons why she was unable to collect all the records of interviews together in one place where the faculty person might have access to them. This all occurred just as my chief assistant and good friend was blowing hot and cold on our own work together. She was either completely present and working with dedication, or (for weeks at a time), completely absent with telephone unplugged and all other means of communication blocked.

These experiences triggered memories even further in the past. For two years, we had run a support group for faculty women, all of whom were highly trained and competent and many of whom were my friends. In general, the group was effective. It provided the ingredients of support: self-confirmation and information exchange. Yet two incidents, contrary to the usual tenor of the group, remain with me. The first was a brief episode when we were discussing future goals for our individual careers. One woman said she would have no part in the discussion because it reflected an undue concern with personal ambition. Another said that she had just put her manuscripts in the drawer and decided *not* to send them to a publisher, because *she* would not sell her soul for success.

The second incident arose when we assigned ourselves the task of placing a woman on every major university committee. It had been clear to some of us that our male colleagues usually negotiated these elections ahead of time. Consequently, enough of them voted as a block to put their preferred candidate in place. They also put up a "sacrificial lamb," usually someone destined to lose, but who would profit from the university-wide visibility. This also-ran usually won the following election.

Some of us suggested that, since there were three positions open, we select three women and choose to back them. At this point, however, seven women had already been nominated to run. It was obvious that if all seven women ran they would split many of the same votes and most likely not win. Therefore, at this meeting, it was proposed that we decide on the three most likely candidates and give them our support. The other four would withdraw their names, or would accept the position of "sacrificial lamb." After long discussion, all the women nominated wanted to run, no one wanted to seriously discuss prospects for success, and in the actual election, all the women lost.

What are the common threads in all these incidents? The graduate students' belief in equality of contribution prevented them from utilizing the expertise of the faculty women. It also prevented them from recognizing and utilizing the different talents among themselves. As a consequence, their program was in jeopardy. The corporate women had a similar interpretation of equality which led them to resent leadership in their group when it emerged in response to a clear need. Where graduate students worked individually with faculty women, there was antagonism and/or separation on the part of the graduate students when status differences could not be concealed. Finally, in the group of faculty women themselves, there was an overt reluctance to discuss "success" or to evaluate one person as potentially more viable for a certain task than another. *In each case, highly-trained and competent women had difficulty recognizing differences of function and status among themselves.*

It would appear that, considering the large number of men at work in high places, there are proportionately fewer who demonstrate similar behavior or who are prey to similar illusions. I have not yet seen a group of men sabotage their own accomplishments in quite the same way or be so reluctant to discuss their own personal goals. I have also not seen a group of men who were so willing to vote themselves out of power by wanting everyone to have an equal chance for a given position. These behaviors are sometimes apparent in individual men, but not in groups of men. The willingness to *not* accomplish tasks, *not* recognize leadership, and *not* plan for strategic action seems to be more common to women than to men.

Returning to the initial discussion of pyramids and circles, it appears that the circular images which are part of women's socialization leads to the behaviors described above. Women are more likely than men to see the world as flat rather than pointed, to see centrality in a group as more important than height. Women are more likely to prefer the intimacy and personal closeness that are associated with a view of life as a series of flat circles than the power and impersonal authority that are associated with life as a series of hierarchical pyramids.

INTEGRATION OF DEMOCRACY
AND HIERARCHY IN ORGANIZATIONS

Both the circular and pyramidal views of groups are necessary for effective group functioning. In the process of forming an effective group it is necessary, at times, to see other human beings as equal, as potential friends and intimates; at other times it is necessary to see them as more or less valued in terms of their particular skills. In order to make this argument, let us distinguish between two primary functions of groups: (1) to provide support, self-confirmation, and information and (2) to accomplish particular tasks. The first function is best served by seeing others as equal to each other within the circular view, the second by viewing others as different from each each other within the pyramidal view.

A group that functions effectively in a circular model will provide support and information to its members. Yet such effective operation requires equality of *function* among group members. Each group member must do similar things, and thus bring similar experience and information to the group. As soon as there is inequality of function, the group will shape itself into a pyramidal structure because some functions will be more essential to the survivial of the group than others. When a circular belief system is imposed on a group which has inequality of function, undercurrents of tension develop which inhibit the operation of the group.

KAFFEE KLATSCH: ALL WOMEN
ARE CREATED EQUAL

As an example, let us follow one group as it evolves from a support circle to a task-oriented pyramid (Figure 9-1). We begin with a stereotypical model: the women's *kaffee klatsch*. Traditionally, women with small children have gathered at a neighbor's house to discuss their children,

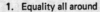
1. Equality all around

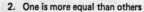
2. One is more equal than others

3. A hierarchy of equals

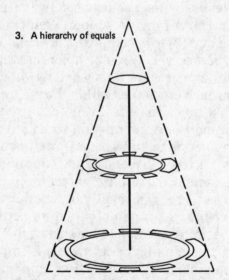

FIGURE 9.1. The first picture represents the circular conversational group; the second is a group with a designated representative; and the third shows the structure formed by the community and neighborhood groups. The expansion of organization occurs in the fourth drawing when new personnel are hired for specific functions, and the group becomes entirely task oriented in the fifth figure when in times of intense productivity.

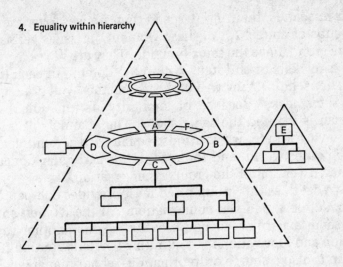

4. Equality within hierarchy

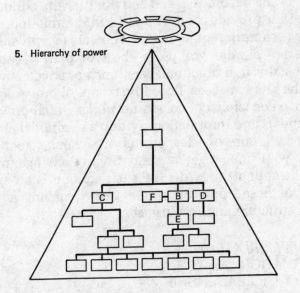

5. Hierarchy of power

FIGURE 9.1. (continued).

133

their husbands, their in-laws, and their houses, over morning cups of coffee. All of these women, on issues germane to the group, have the same function. They are wives to men and caretakers of children. Within the domain of each (her own household), they will perform, whether well or poorly, the same tasks. Because of similarity of function, each woman is granted the same status. The channels of information to the outer world are also equal: Each communicates to the outer world, and to those in her particular domain, a filtered version of the group's conversation.

What does this group provide? It provides companionship, support, and self-confirmation. All the women share the same experiences; they provide for one another satisfaction and motivation for continuing the daily routine. The group is also a source of information—about diapers, cooking, crafts, home decorating, and activities for the children. The group thus provides both support and information, and within the assumption of equality, it operates very well.

There are similar groups in the workplace. Men of equivalent status and function share lunch or an after-work drink for the same purpose. Recently, groups of professional women have consciously evolved networks which provide needed support and information. Within a pyramidal structure, there are groups of salespersons, of research scientists, and others who come together primarily to exchange information. The support provided by such a group is an extra bonus. All of these groups are similar to the women's *kaffee klatsch* in structure and in purpose.

FROM *KAFFEE KLATSCH* TO INFORMATION CENTER: NECESSITY OF LEADERSHIP

Let us suppose this particular group of women who meet for coffee in their own neighborhood comes to the attention of a group in the larger community. The community group hears that these women meet regularly, that they work well with each other personally, and that they provide an information network for each other. The community group is concerned with the fact that many other women, new to the area, have no such source for support and information and, in contrast, feel isolated and alone. Consequently, the larger community group asks the neighborhood women to share their information. The neighborhood women may report regularly to the community organization who can then use this information to begin other support groups for newcomers.

Until now the women in the *kaffee klatsch* have been independent equals. Faced with the request for information from an outside source, however, they choose a person to be their representative. They may have alternate representatives in different months, but they cannot all stop by the community house and convey their bits of information. As a consequence, they must devise an organizational structure for doing this. The person who organizes this structure, whether the representative to the larger group or someone else, will become a leader who is first among equals. All the women in the group still have the same primary function (to care for husbands and children), but some are now more equal than others, because the group's reputation depends on their organizing abilities.

Therefore, as soon as the group becomes tied into a larger system (the community organization), it must shift its own form of organization. Initially operating on a circular model, they shift to a new form, the circular model with a leader (or possibly more than one leader). As soon as there is the need for one voice, one or several members assume a slight ascendancy over the others. This situation is common in committee structures both in the academic and corporate worlds. Academicians meet in committees, often led by a chairperson or a dean, who is regarded as first among equals. Businesspersons who meet, for example, in program committees, are often led by one member who creates the program or contacts outside speakers, thus becoming the first among equals. In general, the person who becomes the leader of such a group, which is still predominantly circular, is the one who is instrumental in seeing that information is conveyed to a larger system.

This, however, is not the only change that has occurred in the women's group. As soon as the group connected with a larger system, they joined a loosely knit hierarchial structure. The group with the smaller scope reports to the one with the greater scope. The smaller circles report to bigger circles who report to bigger circles. The individuals who are instrumental in providing information to other systems have become the almost-equal leaders of each group. The development of leadership is a necessary corollary of any connection with other systems.

CREATION OF A NEWSLETTER: RECOGNITION OF INDIVIDUAL ABILITIES

Returning to the story of the original women's group: They have succeeded in establishing an information link with the community organization which has links to other groups. In the process, however, imagine that the community organization discovers that the original *kaffee klatsch* group represents an untapped pool of talent. The leader of the community organization discovers that one woman has writing experience, one has been an artist, and one was a sales manager for a retail store. She suggests, therefore, that these women organize further to prepare and distribute a monthly newsletter which will go to similar groups throughout the region. In this way, the information and support first shared only by the women in the neighborhood, and later in the larger community, can benefit all women in the region.

In accepting this task, the women's group begins to

assess differing talents to meet differing functions. They select the experienced writer to edit the newspaper, the artist to illustrate it, and the sales manager to supervise distribution. They have created different functions within the group, yet, unwilling to relinquish their circular assumptions, they maintain that all functions, though different, are equal. Unwilling to recognize hierarchy, (in part, for fear they may lose the support that the group has provided) these women still operate as if they were a circular group with a leader who is first among equals.

However, as the production date draws near for the first newsletter, problems arise for individual women. The distributor's children get chicken pox and she is unable to handle the procedures for distributing the paper. The women, however, canvas their neighborhood, and find a college student with sales experience who will complete the task of evolving a distribution system. The college student agrees to work for four dollars per hour. Then the mother of the artist becomes ill and she must fly to another state. The women are unable to find a replacement but decide that the newsletter can be completed without drawings for the first time. Then, the writer's husband is sent on an unexpected business trip to Hawaii and insists that his wife come along. The women attempt to find a replacement but uncover no fledgling writer in their immediate environment. They may hire a semi-professional writer for the cost of fifteen dollars per hour. This is beyond their budget, so they persuade the writer to stay and finish the task and join her husband later. There is some dissension in the writer's household, but she agrees to remain.

As a consequence of these difficulties, the writer's status with the group has increased. As a person who fulfills an indispensible and irreplaceable function, she becomes crucial to the group's success. In terms of function, the distributor is indispensible but replaceable, and the artist is irreplaceable but dispensible. In a disagreement between the writer and the distributor, the group takes the writer's side. Thus, certain people in any task-oriented group assume more importance than others. In light of the goal of task accomplishment, groups develop a hierarchy in which those with the most valued skills are given more authority than others.

In terms of the task of newspaper production, the writer moved to the central position in the group. If the task had been fund-raising, then the person with organizational abilities and affluent connections may be central. If the task is to organize a children's carnival, then a person who likes children and, perhaps, has artistic talent, would become a key figure. The nature of the hierarchy shifts with the task. Yet, it is important to note that the hierarchy need not negate an individual's value as a separate human being. When groups meet for support, individuals such as the writer need have no more primacy than the others. Yet, when groups meet for task accomplishment, the person with the most essential and irreplaceable skills will move front and center.

GROUP SUCCESS: FORMATION OF A HIERARCHY

In the next phase of the *kaffee klatsch's* evolution, they are confronted with a new task. The newspaper is a success and they are asked if they would produce a quarterly newspaper for the entire state. For this venture, they will be paid by a specific state agency which supports community groups. After accepting this challenge, they must, therefore, decide on appropriate salaries. They must hire people who will report directly to the person whose function they extend. For example, they will hire reporters who work with the writer. They will hire teenagers to report to the distributor.

They will solicit work from fledgling artists who will consult with the group's artist. Finally, one person may be appointed to hire and supervise all of these people. With this last step, the women have evolved a hierarchical organization, with employees reporting to supervisors, with staff (personnel) and line (production) functions. From the circular model, the women have moved to a hierarchical mode. Yet, the women still meet on occasional weekdays in their old circular form to discuss problems and share information.

The evolution of such a group, however, is a rare occurrence. Once bred to one model, groups have difficulty evolving another. The models, instead of compatible alternatives, are often seen as competitive with each other, the one supplanting and suppressing the other. Hence it is assumed, most often by women, that a support group cannot evolve a hierarchical structure without losing the support and confirmation functions for which it was originally designed. It is also assumed, most often by men, that hierarchical models must, of necessity, be imposed on all work and personal relationships, thus denying men the closeness, intimacy, and support which they require as human beings. Occasional individuals and occasional groups, however, learn that the full function of many groups is best facilitated by a combination of the two organizational models.

In the example given in the beginning of this chapter, we saw many women's groups struggling not to recognize the necessity for hierarchy. Hence, whereas these groups may function well in supportive areas, they bog down when confronted with demands for task accomplishment. Faced with a desirable and immediate goal, however, unrecognized leadership may emerge to meet pressing needs. Yet, if this occurs the group may punish the person who took on leadership functions because she deviated from the circular model. On the other hand, where status and function differences already exist, these may be ignored as women seek equality and companionship. When recognition of these differences is inescapable, however, women may abandon the bond which has been built on the premise of equality. Or, finally, in more subtle ways, women may act against each other to discriminate against those who have acquired status or who have assumed leadership.

The world is, however, composed of neither circles nor pyramids alone. Throughout the hierarchical world, circles emerge which provide the necessary support and information to sustain human beings. And, in the midst of the flat circular world, pyramids will grow when faced with the necessity of getting something done. The circles provide us with horizontal networks. The pyramids provide us with vertical networks. Living in a multidimensional world, it is necessary that we correctly characterize the space we live in. In and out, up and down, both dimensions extend the scope of the individual, and in turn provide the necessary arenas for the development of power and love.

CHAPTER TEN

CREATIVE
PRODUCTIVITY:
THE USES OF POWER

Many of us may have come to terms with the need to accept both hierarchical and circular frameworks in the workplace. We may intellectually grasp the benefits of operating in the realms of both power and love. Yet for many of us who understand these concepts on an intellectual level, it is still difficult to enact them in our everyday organizational world. We may accept the possibility that we ought to create a vertical and horizontal space for ourselves within our organizational system. We might recognize that such might be the best use of our time and energy in a creatively productive way. Yet, this conceptual acceptance may provide small comfort in the realities of the workplace where individuals are often discontent. How can we use our knowledge to increase our own satisfaction and the productivity of the systems in which we live and work? In other words, how do we implement our awareness of the realities of power (and love) in order to be creatively productive?

The issue in the workplace is predominantly one of power. Although power is not effective without love, the realities of this world revolve around the hierarchical structure which is part of the world of power. Furthermore, it is in terms of power that individuals most often evaluate themselves negatively in the organizational sphere. Individuals often say, "*They* do not recognize *my* talents"; others complain "My boss expects too much of me." What they are really saying is that they experience themselves at the mercy of others. In the world's balance of power, they perceive themselves on the short end of the stick. They see themselves as powerless and make this the chief measure of their being.

I believe, however, that an individual has the capacity to change the balance and right the equation by taking control of her own life. Within the work world the individual can find the appropriate slot where individual talents are in synchrony with organizational expectations. By not accepting her lot as given, an individual can "negotiate the system" until she finds a satisfactory niche. As she does so, she discovers that not everything which seems to be a roadblock really is, and that barriers can be shown to have gates and passageways not previously apparent. In general, to become creatively productive requires knowledge, planning, and action. The knowledge required lies in three areas: (1) knowledge of the self, (2) knowledge of the system, and (3) knowledge of potential career paths, the places in which the self and system meet. In each of these three areas, our knowledge tends to be simplistic and unrealistic. We fail to acknowledge the complexities and contradictions that exist within the self, within the system, and within our career paths. The contradictions make clear-cut planning difficult, but also open the way for alternative courses of action which we may have overlooked.

UNDERSTANDING THE SELF

In terms of the individual, it is useful to think of the self as a system, composed of many interrelated parts. In this way, we can recognize the many parts of the self, some of which are in agreement with each other, some of which are opposed to each other. Thus, the self is both complex and contradictory. For example, when a man says, "I want . . .," it is most likely that he could as easily have said, "I don't want . . ." Most of the things we desire, we also do not desire. Often part of us wants to do something while part of us does not. We are pulled between two currents, one going forward and the other going backward. We want to move ahead and take the risks of the unknown, and we want to stay behind, safe in the familiar confines of our given world.

This dual tendency of human beings to want to try new things and to avoid new things is part of the individual's complexity. Yet, we often tell ourselves, "I have to want it completely, I have to be sure." How sure is sure? Human beings are at least a little bit scared of almost everything. Most people I know want to leave their marriages at least once in a while, and want to stay in them the rest of the time. The same people have days when they would give anything to have a different job, and yet on other days they are delighted with their work environment. The push-and-pull of human life expresses itself in many different forms. Nothing is clear and simple.

When we believe that what we want is clear and simple, we may in fact express mixed messages to others in the world. We may believe, simplistically, that "Yes, I want that promotion." We may convey that to our superior. Yet, another part of ourselves, which we are choosing not to recognize, is saying something quite different, such as, "But maybe I can't do the work, maybe I won't have anybody to talk to in the new office, maybe . . . maybe . . . maybe . . . I won't make it." And out ahead looms the threat of potential failure. Or, perhaps, for some, out ahead looms the threat of potential success: "If I make it, nobody will like me and I'll lose all my friends, or I'll have surpassed my father or my mother." The ultimate fear is "I have to take responsibility for myself."

Human beings are a funny mix of certainties and doubts. We are often scared. We do not like it where we are. We do not want to move ahead because it may be worse. We dare not fall behind because then we really will have failed. And yet, when we do not recognize all of this in ourselves, and we say to our boss, "Yes, I want that promotion," with our voice, our head, our smile, or perhaps the wiggle of our foot, we are also saying, "But, I'm not so sure about that." One of the results, therefore, of not acknowledging all of ourselves is that we often do not say what we mean, and our nonverbal behavior is saying it for us. Others tune in on the nonverbal wavelength, often without consciousness, and say, "But do you really want the job?" Or, perhaps, they will not say it, but will lose the papers, forget to fill out the proper forms, and with the passage of time, the opportunity is lost.

So it becomes very important to recognize all parts of the self. This does not mean that one then explains to one's superior, "Yes, I want the job, but, you see, I have these doubts . . . so you decide for me." Rather, one recognizes all these inner messages, weighs the pros and cons of familiarity and adventure, of success and failure, and makes a strategic choice—and a commitment. Given the knowledge of self, one chooses fully, knowing that no choice is ever simple and clearcut and that there are ambiguities which one can deal with, rather than allowing others to decide them for us. So we might say, "Yes, I want the promotion. I've really thought about it and I believe I can handle the work, and I will appreciate the challenge." Having recognized all parts of self in making this decision, we give off only one message. Surprisingly, the superior is less likely to lose the papers and forget the forms—and often, but not always, the promotion comes through.

We may thus experience ourselves as very complex in the present. We did not, however, emerge fullblown at this moment in time, but we have also a past and a future. We also learn something about our future possibilities from our past history. Many of the regrettable decisions made by human beings are made because we are thinking of what we want *now*, what feels good (or bad) at this moment in time, and what would enhance our sense of well-being at the moment. If those same decisions had been looked at in the framework of a five-, ten- or twenty-year timespan, we might have chosen differently. If all of us lived this way, our pollution problem would be minimal, our economy would be in better shape, and our industrial and educational institutions might have grown beyond a stopgap philosophy.

Yet, in our own thinking, you and I can incorporate a time frame into our view of ourselves. One of the ways to sort out the complexities of the self is to look for continuities over time. Perhaps today you are 75% sure you would like to remain in your current job and 25% unsure. Look over the last two years. Have you generally been content with stable and familiar surroundings? Or were you always looking for excitement if things got a little dull? (Always means about 75% of the time, never *all* the time.) Have you in the past volunteered for more responsibilities? Have you done them relatively well? Within human beings, there are not only contradictions, but continuities. What are yours? These continuities are, though subject to change, a good basis on which to begin an exploration of self.

Having searched for continuities, we must remember that what we do today has an impact on tomorrow. If you give up an opportunity now, where will you be in five years? You may or may not like the alternatives. If you let something go that might be done today, will you have a whole roomful of undone tasks to face in five years? A realistic look at our future often provides the motivation for action. Standing still may be comfortable at the moment, but the square you are standing still on may seem much smaller in five years as the rest of the world rolls by. Familiarity is often as poor a choice as is the unknown. The tendency to choose the familiar in all situations (not just some) diminishes when we take a long look down the road along which the familiar will take us. Thus, weighed over time, our decisions become more realistic. They never become more certain, for there is no certainty. But, at least, we are aware of alternatives and their consequences. We are more prepared to accept the consequences as of our own choosing, since we have forseen their possibility.

In the past, then, we may search for continuities. In the future, we project alternatives. The complex self examines itself in time. Beyond this, however, the self also lives in a system. In fact, the self lives in a number of overlapping systems. Whereas the self may be viewed as a system, it is but a part of many larger systems. Any action that we take, therefore, affects others in the systems in which we work and live.

The recognition that we live in systems is an important one. It is also one that we often ignore. For example, one woman said to me, "If I could do exactly what I wanted to, I would work twenty hours a day, and not ever clean house nor cook dinner." What she is really saying is, "If I lived in a vacuum, without others . . ." None of us lives in a vacuum. We are where we are because of our parents, our schools, our legal institutions, and so forth. Even if we go out into the woods to live in a cabin, we are dependent on forest rangers, food producers, and those who make tools and other necessities. We always live in systems.

Yet individuals often talk as if they existed independently. "If it weren't for my wife, I'd go fishing every day," says one man. "If it weren't for my secretaries botching things up, this job would have been finished," says another. Such comments reflect an "I vs. They" thinking. I would do it right, have fun, make a million dollars, if it weren't for them—wives, husbands, bosses, secretaries, the government, and the rest of the world. Yet *they* compose the system in which we live. The "I" is not separate from the "They." Rather the "I" plus the "They" make "We," a "We" which is part of an interdependent world.

Instead, what individuals are reflecting when they talk of "I" and "They" is a conflict of interest and desires within an interdependent system. Just as the self is contradictory, so are systems contradictory. Individual parts often do not want the same thing, nor move toward the same goal. Just as with the self, the system is composed of many parts, which can be reconciled only when we recognize the contradictions, search for continuities over time, and project alternatives into the future.

Just like individuals, systems have goals and directions. They move in a certain way. Some have goals which we could not agree with. Others have goals which are compatible with our own. They move toward these goals, sometimes in an erratic way, and sometimes they appear not to move at all. Yet if the system's goals are congruent with the individual's goals, often the immediacy of particular conflicts can be lessened by recognizing the larger and long-range goals of both the self and the system.

For example, a marriage—which is a personal system—may have as goals the well-being of both partners and the healthy development of the children. Immediate conflict may arise, however, over how to spend vacation time or extra money. (Having extra of anything—welcomed as it is—often provokes dissension because it introduces a greater degree of choice.) Suppose the man wants to go fishing in the mountains, and the woman wants a vacation on the ocean. Each feels that the other is the "They" which is inhibiting the choice of the "I." Yet, what are the goals of the system in this instance? Relaxation and recreation for both individuals and for their children. Can this be accomplished in either place? Probably so. Yet, if the woman agrees to go to the mountains, (or the man to the beach) and feels resentful, this will interfere with the rest and relaxation of all parties, the common goal.

How does one deal with resentment in this instance? By recognizing the interplay of self and system over time. In this case, the system benefits from both partners' agreeing on a place to go, and neither being resentful and thus sabotaging the purpose of the excursion. Hence, the woman (in this case) may agree to go (quite happily) to the mountains. Her individual goals yield to the larger needs of the system. But, the system would not be functioning well if this were always the case. There are other times when her goals and the system's goals are in accord. For example, she has recently returned to graduate school in the evenings in order to further her chances of promotion at work. In this case, her own desires merge with that of the system which functions better when both partners are meeting their long-term goals (and also earning enough money to support the system). In a viable interchange between self and system, most of the time individual goals accord with systems goals; when they do not, if the issue is not a lifetime priority, the individual may yield with grace.

In an institutional system, such as a corporation, the same interplay between self and system occurs. In many institutions today, there are budget cuts (and sometimes personnel cuts) due to difficult economic times. In one system, managerial employees may be asked to reduce their expense accounts by half in order to meet a more stringent budget. One middle manager may resent this because he is missing his yearly business trip to Florida which is also a pleasure trip. He complains to his friends: "If *they* had any sense . . ." Yet *they* are working, however effectively, to keep the system going, the same system which pays the manager's salary and provides him with a good income for himself and his family. If the larger system were not to survive, he would indeed be in a bad place. Yet, in order for systems to survive, individuals must sometimes yield on personal desires. From this viewpoint, it is easier for the middle manager to accept the loss of his trip to Florida. (That is, it is easier unless this particular manager believes that the money is going into his boss's pocket. Then he may be justified in feeling resentful, for neither he nor the boss is recognizing the importance of the larger system and are, indeed, engaging in an "I vs. They" tug-of-war.)

In summary, the complex self is part of a complex larger system (many larger systems) which exist over time, and are themselves part of even larger systems. Thus, within this framework (if one does not boggle at the sheer enormity of it), one may lay the foundations for decision-making which goes beyond the immediate. Yet, just as the self exists on a number of levels, so do systems. Just as the self may say one thing and do another, so do systems often write down for public view one thing, and do quite another. We turn now to the second task, the exploration of the system.

UNDERSTANDING THE SYSTEM

In examining the nature of systems, we speak of any group of individuals brought together for a purpose, large or small. These individuals may be interdependent with each other within personal or impersonal systems. Personal systems are those, like marriage, which are generally founded on shared experiences and mutual affection or respect. The glue of personal systems is, therefore, emotional, at least on one level. In what is called the private sector of our world we are part of many personal systems: the family, the neighborhood, the community, various clubs and associations. Although we may be part of formal systems which are held together by rules, regulations, and procedures, in what is termed the public sphere, it is the glue of the private sector, affection and respect, which still makes the public world go around. This global statement requires considerable clarification.

Public systems, often called *formal* systems, are those which exist in our institutions, whether they are governmental, industrial or educational. All of these public systems have guidelines which are written on paper and printed as part of the public domain. These guidelines include organizational charts (which tell who is in a position of power and who is not), employee policies (which detail the responsibilities of those who work in institutions), and various other paraphernalia relating to the procedures of the workplace. One of the most common causes of personal defeat in organizations, however, lies in believing that these paper rules describe what *is*, and expecting that things work as they are laid out on paper.

The reason that they do not work is that public systems, formalized and written down, are permeated by private or *informal* systems which are never written down. The business of institutions passes through the linkages created by people who went to the same school, who root for the same team, who go deer-hunting at the same time each season, who are married into the same family, or who attend the same church. Groups which share interests and experiences talk among each other more than individuals formally collected in a system by an organizational structure. As they talk among each other, business is transacted. The linkages formed by personal systems are often referred to as the "old boys' network." What they do when they are together, or what they say about those in other systems than their own, is often called "office politics."

This is the heart of the informal system in all organizations: This is not where things are supposed to happen, but it is where they do happen. You may read about how it is supposed to be, but you can only find out how it is by watching and listening. Who talks to whom and when? Who visits with whom? What groups eat lunch together, go to the water cooler together? From observation, one can determine how the system operates and who makes the decisions. Often, it is true, the organizational chart may approximate the informal power system. But there are always exceptions, the supposedly powerful person who does practically nothing, and the behind the scenes "mover and shaker."

Having identified the larger informal system in your organization, examine your own informal systems. Whom do you talk to most, how often, and why? Are these people "like you" who can understand your work and your problems and will feed you the information you need as it comes down the pipeline? This is your horizontal network. Then, are there people whom you talk with who have more "clout" than you do? Are there people who have a communication channel to the top? And then, are there people who are less powerful than you who are supporting you, perhaps being trained to move up as you move up? This is your vertical network.

The next step is to assess your systems in terms of their adequacy. Do you have enough people to talk to about your problems? Do you have a pipeline to the top when you want visibility or when you need action? If your systems are adequate, then you put energy into maintaining them. If they are inadequate, then you put energy into strengthening them. To acquire more ties with the top, you find out what the powerful are interested in, and find time to listen to them talk about it. Or, you may develop projects which are in line with their interests and ask for assistance in promotion of your project. If this project meets both their needs and yours, you have found a way to bring congruence into the interplay between self and system.

Then, put some energy into your relationships with

your subordinates. They are the foundation on which you rise or fall. Listen to them, take time to hear their problems, and to honor their successes. Delegate tasks carefully, so those who work for you are neither ignored nor overburdened. Respect their right to work in their own way as long as goals are accomplished. Finally, take time to be with your peers, to confirm their sense of self. Then you will have allies who will support you in your next moves, to help you gain the information, visibility, and recognition which you need to continue negotiating the system. When you have a functioning informal system of your own, which interconnects with the informal system of your workplace, then you are part of the interconnected network of individuals who make the system move ahead—or stop.

UNDERSTANDING YOUR CAREER PATH: SELF AND SYSTEM

Finally, we turn to the place where self and system come together, your career path. This is a path, a direction, and not a station. It is a journey that you are on and not a place where you have arrived. The interface of the self and system is a constantly changing course, both continuous and discontinuous from one stage to the next. When we are at odds with ourselves and our system, we may perceive our career paths as static. We may feel we are occupying a continually shrinking zone where we do the same work over and over, for years and years. We may feel boxed in, thwarted, finding every doorway is but a mirage in an impassable wall. We may feel peripheral, outside, not a part of the larger system but clinging to the edge. Or, again, we may find ourselves system-hopping, as one system edges us out and we move to another, repeating the same process again and again.

In each of these situations, there is a familiar pattern

which operates repeatedly. Regardless of changes, one may act the same and find familiarity in an unchanging sequence of behavior. The fact that these patterns repeat themselves reflects an avoidance of change. The world has changed and gone forward. Though the places and faces may differ, if our situation is always the same, then we have established sameness in a changing world. We may behave the same way regardless of whether the situation is old or new. We may avoid change by keeping our situation as familiar as possible, or by enacting the same behavior patterns time and time again. All of these solutions (for they may appear to be so) arise from a lack of balance between the self and the system, and perhaps an unrealistic appraisal of each.

The solution which makes more sense is to recognize that the world is changing and so must we. We can move with change, plan for change, and thus negotiate our systems. In this way, we are creative and productive, and we use our power well. We are in control, not "They," the "They" then becomes only one of us. Knowing who we are, what our systems are like, and what our desired career paths are, we can move toward our goals over time. Having made commitments to a plan of action, we can test it out and evaluate the responses. In evaluation, we may modify but not throw out our plans. We adapt them, instead, to our new information. When we recognize and move with change, less of our energy goes into resentment and confusion. When we recognize too the importance of the larger systems in which we live as well as the complexities of the self, we can plan realistically for a changing world.

As we do this, we need to remember that Americans have a myth about success. They assume (we assume?) that everyone wants to go upward. Nonsense. Some of us really want to stay where we are, but even that requires that we adapt and grow as we recognize that times and circumstances change. Some want to move to the top—or have a shot at it—and are willing to assume the risks which such action requires. We need to assess ourselves carefully, without a mythology of "going up"; we must learn to negotiate the system whether we are going up, down, or standing still—for even that will change.

To summarize, individuals who increase their sense of power in the workplace have an understanding of themselves, the systems in which they work, and their career paths. They recognize the complexity and contradictions of self. They are willing to make use of what they have done in the past and create new directions for the future. Accepting themselves as complex and living in time, they make choices and commitments which are in line both with the past continuities of their lives as well as future directions. They are, moreover, willing to commit themselves to these choices, plan for a period of time, and reevaluate the results and perhaps modify their choices.

Further, they are aware that the systems in which they live are complex. They pay attention both to the formal system and the informal one. They watch and listen and learn how the system operates and then choose how they will become part of that system. They get to know others, they recognize the value of their subordinates, and they respect the status of their superiors. Yet, they do not rely on the "paper system" created for public view, but acknowledge and accept and utilize the networks of connections which exist in the private world beyond the public's gaze.

Finally, they plan their career path to take into account both the realities of the self and of the system. They "negotiate the system," until they find the position which best matches their own talents. Individuals in such positions do not complain of their lack of power. Nor do these individuals seek only to be acknowledged by others; rather, by relying on their own sense of strength, they reach out to others. In this way they bring together the worlds of power and love. Such individuals are creatively productive, and their work contributes to their own well-being and to the effectiveness of the systems in which they work.

PART IV

BEYOND POWER AND LOVE

CHAPTER ELEVEN

THE EXPERIENCE OF TRUTH: KNOWING THE UNKNOWABLE

Throughout this book the emphasis has been on the integration of the two dimensions of human existence, power and love. In our human world, in which our personal desires and those of others come into play, power and love often represent polarities in our lives. We want to be autonomous and do our own thing (power) and we want to be intimate with others and be part of their lives (love). We want to know who we are and communicate it to the world (power) and we want to find out who others are and confirm their sense of self (love). The differing ways in which we resolve these issues at different stages of life define the thematic content of our lives. At each stage of life, we may find a new resolution of the push-and-pull between power and love. Yet each resolution must be tested again in the context of the new issues which emerge with a new developmental stage.

In a traditional pattern, for instance, an adolescent with a newfound sense of self may then struggle to maintain this sense of self in close association with a boyfriend or girl friend. With some sense of resolution of the self-other issue, young persons may approach their twenties, in which the sense of self and the creation of an intimate partnership must withstand the demands of both children and work. The self (power) and other (love) conflict has emerged in a larger sphere which includes responsibilities toward many more people than before. Later in life, the conflict takes a new form as one lets go of the family ties which have defined the self to venture into new fields and new associations. Again, the sense of self (power) may be threatened by the desire to meet the demands and expectations of others (love). The continual interplay of power and love throughout life encompasses most of the conflicts which define and give form to the human experience.

The power and love conflict assumes importance in any stage of life because human beings have personal desires and live in community with others. We are interconnected with others who have their own desires, hopes, and expectations. Living in a social world, however, we are limited in time and space. Our energy cannot be divided up to meet all expectations and all demands. Instead, in our everyday world, we must devote so much energy to one thing (person) and not to another. We have commitments from the past which guide our choices in the future. We are not free at any moment to do exactly as we please or just as others would wish. The limitations of our world require that we choose and, generally, the choices that we make reflect the importance which we give to either power or love in that time of our life. Sometimes, it is entirely possible, we may find a resolution of the conflict between power and love and achieve a balance of the two. The balance, however, is continually tested. The next development in our lives may challenge the equilibrium we have reached. Thus, even if we are both powerful and loving at one time of life, the continuing balance of the two is never assured.

The universe, however, is not defined by the human world. There are expanses we do not know. Scientists shoot space probes into the universe and rejoice when we have discovered fragments of knowledge. Mystics and seers have visions of this universe and give descriptions of what cannot be described. Great philosophers sketch some of the pathways through the intellectual circuits of this unknown sphere. The universe, whether viewed by science, religion, or philosophy, cannot be comprehended by our intellect. It is unknowable. In the context of the universal, that which we know is a small part of the possible and our intellectualizing is child's play.

Against this backdrop, the concepts created by intellect must also diminish in importance. Power and love, important in our personal and social spheres, may matter little in terms of the great unknown. In this larger context, it is possible that power and love are not separate but as one, part of the pulsation of some universal vibration which enlivens all things.

If we accept the possibility of limited knowledge, then how does one live in this world? Does one give up judging, choosing, taking action? Does one yield to one's momentary desires since there is no certainty in any given course? We might suppose then that being both powerful and loving is no guarantee of health or wealth of wisdom. What then is our standard for choosing courses of action? Psychological portraits of maturity can answer these questions in part. In the lives of those who choose, who act, who develop their talents fully, there is evidence of greater vitality and stronger interpersonal relationships. In the lives of those who drift, who go with their momentary desires, there appear to be less of all of these characteristics. Indeed there are no guarantees, but there is evidence to suggest that choosing and being committed to a certain course often enhances individual lives.

THE PLACE OF REASON
IN OUR LIVES

In the lives of those people whom I admire (some from my own experience and some from books) there appear to be some constants. Such people have often shed the superficial trappings that they have acquired in this life. They have learned to let go of their "personal history," and are thus less trapped by their own past. As a consequence, they live more fully in the present. But this is not the present of the drifter who is moved by momentary desires. Rather these highly developed people respond clearly to their environment (and the people in it) as it is—without being imprisoned by the patterns of their past. These people always see the world with fresh eyes. They are not jaded, cynical, or defeated. Rather they welcome each moment as it arrives.

In part, they do so because they sense a wider panorama beyond their vision. In the larger scope of things, they perceive the unimportance of their immediate needs, their past failures, and their future hopes. Their sense of self is thus tempered by a recognition of their own insignificance. *Unreasonably*, this sense of insignificance allows a fuller awareness of immediate significance to spring forth. *Contrary to reason*, in perceiving that what they do does not matter all that much, the immediate impact of their actions is handled with more care, more responsibility, and more concern for others. In the larger scope of things, what they happen to want at any moment matters less than how they affect others in what they do. Thus, their victories are not all-encompassing and their defeats are not total. Both victory and defeat reflect only a very partial truth. Fully aware of their limitations, yet sensing their own aliveness, these individuals temper judgment with mercy and evaluation with compassion. Actively engaged in the personal and social world, they are vitalized by an energy which springs from some universal well of human interconnection.

In order to do so, however, they must sometimes abandon the path of reason. Our logical explorations may take us to the door of the universal world, and beyond human knowledge, but we may enter only when we "let go" and allow our inner wisdom to guide our rationality. Reason is our companion in life but it cannot always be our guide. The path of reason, of logic, is to explore all alternatives. The answer to the larger issues of life and death may appear only outside the path of reason when we let go of the limitations of our rationality. Bound within our human universe, reason is a tool of our personal and social world. The sense of vitality engendered by contact with the universal sphere emerges spontaneously when the search is given over and reason is set aside.

All human theories, including that of power and love, are drawn within human limitations and are colored by the personal nature of our pallets. The integration of power and love may pull together the polarities of our human, finite existence. Having achieved this integration, we then approach another world, a universal timeless sphere, which reminds us of the partialness of what we know and the great expanse of that which lies beyond our knowledge.

The framework which we choose as our own to guide our course in life, however limited by our own finitude, must still be large enough to give full scope to the range of human potential. If the screen against which we cast ourselves is big enough, we will save our energies for the larger issues in human lives. If we choose instead to shelter ourselves within a framework fit for a toadstool, we may find our energies absorbed by small issues, no bigger than a blade of grass. Thus, it is important to develop an encompassing framework for human lives and let it form the basis of our orientation toward others and our world. Such a framework will not provide the final answers but it will give us a direction and provide a far-ranging backdrop against which to assess the major questions of human life.

On one level, the framework presented in this book, the integration of power and love, can encompass the scope of human life and point us in the direction of universal concerns. Accepting the challenge to become both powerful and loving may enlarge our personal potential and provide opportunities for the vitality and strength engendered by a sense of the universal.

CONCLUSION

These last pages stand as cautionary notes at the end of this book. They serve as question marks in my own mind which preclude finality on any of the issues addressed previously. In the human world, as I know it, most of what we do, and most of the conflicts that we experience, can be reduced to the basic conflict that we experience between power and love. In this world, too, the people whom I admire, who stand as models for me, are those who both do things and care about people, and both their doing and their caring are evident to many who know them. In my own life, when I feel "out of synchrony," it is often because the balance of power and love has gone awry and I am experiencing myself as either powerless or unloving (and unloved). I am aware, however, in my conversations with other friends and associates that there are so many unanswered questions in the universe, and so much that we do not know about people, that my conclusions on these matters are subject to change— and, that, in moments of wider vision, some of this may not matter much at all.

The underlying message is it is hard for me to put a period to anything. I sit here drawing this out. But, this is a book about change and about transition—and the fact that I find myself always aware of transition is appropriate in this context. Let me summarize by reemphasizing the importance of the dual themes of power and love: They wind their way throughout our lives and provide a framework for understanding the developmental paths of males and females, their relationships to each other, and their cooperation and competition in the world of work. Yet we must temper this awareness with the vision of worlds beyond our ken and the requirement that in this sea of uncertainty we yet must choose.

EPILOGUE:
THE RIGHT TO GROW

PART ONE

Once upon a time in a land called Wizzledom the misty purplish-pink air which hung over the fruitful gardens and placid hearths began to turn an unpleasant shade of purplish-blue as the inhabitants of the land, the Wizzles and the Quizzles, found themselves beset by inner strife. Now this darkening of the mists first came about when the Wizzles, who professed equality of all beings whether rectangular or spherical, green, orange, or yellow, kindly (but not too seriously) bestowed upon the Quizzles the right to share in the major task of the land, the growing of the red Arpanzees.

Traditionally, Arpanzees had been grown only by the Wizzles who found the work hard and troublesome (or said that they did) and consequently were justly served (or so they said) by the Quizzles who did everything else in the land of Wizzledom, most particularly the condensing of Arpanzees for the daily meal. This state of affairs had gone on for so long that its beginning was said to lie beyond the edge of the purplish-pink sky and thus outside the knowledge of any being, whether Wizzle or Quizzle. In fact, it had gone on for so long that none could remember, and only a few could entertain the possibility of another way of life; there were hints that Wizzles growing and Quizzles condensing was the natural order of things. Some even said, though nobody said it seriously, that if this order of things were disturbed the world would go up in a giant fizzle!

Yet among the inhabitants of Wizzledom there were some, primarily Quizzles, who were restive and energetic and who, timidly at first but then more strongly, began to question this order of things. The Wizzles (not all, but a noticeable number of them) naturally looked at these Quizzles to see if they were losing their spherical shape or their orange color, for surely normal Quizzles would never think of such a thing! However, these Quizzles were both spherical and orange (all Quizzles should be: the better for stirring pots and sitting on stools, they say) and did not show any outward signs of the strange transformations they were undergoing. As these restive Quizzles questioned and thought, other Quizzles joined them. Together they all questioned and thought, and many came to the same idea all at once: Maybe growing Arpanzees might be more fun than sitting and condensing!

When the Wizzles heard them say this, many trembled with apprehension, although they did not know why. The Wizzles maintained that growing Arpanzees was very hard work; certainly they had complained enough so that everybody knew that? But—and here the Wizzles straightened their rectangular shoulders and puffed up their yellow bodies—if the Quizzles should want to share in such burdensome toil, that was certainly their privilege since this was a land of equality. Thus the Wizzles came to grant the Quizzles the right to grow, while whispering and winking among themsleves that the Quizzles would soon tire of such hard work and return to the softer task of condensing Arpanzees. It was shortly after this that the purplish-pink skies began to turn purplish-blue and there was a new uneasiness in the land.

This change in the mists came about when it was observed that indeed some Quizzles did enjoy growing Arpanzees. Although many Quizzles who tried their round hands at growing soon returned to the pots, there were some Quizzles who continued to tend their gardens. These Quizzles did not seem to be dismayed by the puzzlement of the Wizzles with whom they lived side by side and they continued to turn the earth, to sow the seed, and to grow.

These Quizzles also were not upset—at least initially— by the actions of some of the puzzled Wizzles. Now the Wizzles were not doing anything much, of course, for the Wizzles did believe that everyone had the right to do whatever it pleased in this land of equality (or so they said). Yet these Wizzles had inadvertently managed to track Wizzledust across the gardens of the Quizzles; Wizzledust is very sharp and thistly and prevents the Arpanzees from peeking their red heads out of the ground. Moreover, these same Wizzles pointed out from time to time how the hearths were being neglected, the condensing was less than it might be, and the little Wizzles of the land (who later would be distinguished as Wizzles and Quizzles) were running wild across all the gardens rather than being watched near the condensing pots. The Wizzles were even overheard saying, when they thought no Quizzles were about, that the world was about to go up in a giant fizzle! And even though they maintained publicly that they were quite content with the new state of affairs, the sky over Wizzledom turned a darker shade of blue.

As the Wizzles continued to do nothing much in this fashion, and the purplish-blue mists continued to hang over Wizzledom, many Quizzles who had remained in the fields became disheartened by the new blue tone of things and retreated to their hearths and their pots, intoning the ancient saying that after all round bottoms are for stool-sitting and square ones for seed-sowing and it was perfectly obvious what spherical and rectangular had been made to do.

However, here and there a few Quizzles persevered and found that growing Arpanzees was indeed fun, despite the Wizzledust tracked across their gardens and despite the untended pots (or rather not-as-well-tended pots as formerly). These Quizzles said it was exciting to see the little red heads poke out of the ground, to see the first orange leaves reach toward the sun, to watch the red, orange, and yellow plant grow to fruition and to harvest them for the daily pots. These Quizzles seemed not to notice the blueness of things, so engrossed were they in their new undertaking. They saw no reason to return to the hearth.

Nonetheless, as time progressed, some of these Quizzles found their work becoming harder and harder. These Quizzles missed the daily company of other Quizzles and found it difficult to talk with the Wizzles, who generally acted as if they were not there. These Quizzles also found little seeds of doubt within themselves and did not know if they were still natural Quizzles after all. They felt hurt that the Wizzles would not talk to them and they were upset by the condescending attitude of the hearthbound Quizzles who said that growing Quizzles were dirtying their hands in the garden and, after all, everybody knew (very secretly) that condensing led to the virtue of cleanliness which Quizzles valued above all else (or so they said).

These growing Quizzles, the ones who nourished the seeds of doubt, were indeed having quite a time of it. There were other difficulties as well. These growing Quizzles were also condensing (though not very well as everyone knew), since there was no one else to condense for them and thus they were doing two jobs at once which tired them out considerably and no one could possibly do well at two jobs (or so everyone said). (It is true that, to some extent, they brought this problem upon themselves. There were a few unusual Wizzles who offered to help with the condensing and the Quizzles said "No!"—a most surprising reply, which shows that it was not only the Wizzles who were hung up on the natural order of things.)

But the major problem that the Quizzles faced was the Wizzledust tracked across the Quizzles' gardens. Yet despite doubts and Wizzledust, many Quizzles continued to grow. Oranzee was one such Quizzle, who had fewer doubts than many others, and who took such delight in its garden that it had little difficulty returning to the hearth and condensing its dinner and even sometimes allowed a Wizzle to help it out. Oranzee did not even mind whisking away the Wizzledust tracked across its garden each day at the Panzee Hour (the time of the noonday meal) before hurrying to the hearth and pots to condense its own Arpanzees. However, not all the problems of this world are of our own creation: One day, instead of one Wizzle tracking Wizzledust across its garden, two Wizzles tracked dust across and the Arpanzees almost tucked their heads back under the ground. Oranzee was at that moment a little tired and quite dismayed and feeling very blue and said to the Wizzles:

"Oh, please, would you walk around my garden? Don't you see that you are tracking Wizzledust just all over the place?"

The Wizzles smiled, said they were so sorry, tweaked Oranzee's ear, patted it on the back, and said:

"Well, this is hard work for a Quizzle anyway. We wouldn't want to make it any more difficult. We will try to be more careful but if you don't like it, why don't you go tend your pots?"

They snickered to each other and trotted off to their daily meal. Oranzee felt angry but did not know why. After all, the Wizzles had really been quite nice about everything.

So it brushed the Wizzledust away from the Arpanzees, gathered up its tools, and went home to tend the pots for its midday meal—half a noon-hour late.

The next day, three Wizzles tracked their way across Oranzee's garden leaving a large amount of Wizzledust in their wake. Oranzee was astonished, its face turned from orange to green. Its mouth opened and it said:

"What are you doing that for? I thought you said you were sorry!"

The Wizzles feigned surprise, laughed, tweaked Oranzee's ear and patted its back, and said:

"Oh, we were so careless. We forgot. It's just so surprising to find a Quizzle doing Wizzle's work that we forget that *this* is a *garden!*"

Again they laughed among themselves and trotted off to their noonday meal.

Again Oranzee was angry but decided that it just did not understand the Wizzles' world and that it must just work that much harder. So instead of eating its daily meal, it spent the next hour removing all the Wizzledust from the garden so that the Arpanzees untucked their heads and rose sturdily once more reaching for the sun.

"It's all worth it," Oranzee thought pushing away blue thoughts and regarding its bright red Arpanzees. "But I must learn the ways of the gardens. Perhaps I am doing something wrong. I must watch and see how Wizzles handle this problem." (One can see that, at this point, even in Oranzee the seeds of self-doubt were growing; even energetic Quizzles sometimes succumb to typical spherical feelings.)

But Oranzee watched and watched and did not see any Wizzles track Wizzledust across each other's gardens. Yet Wizzles continued to track Wizzledust across *its* garden and Oranzee continued to work three times as hard as anybody else so that its garden might flourish. Each day it gave up eating at Panzee Hour so that it could clear off the Wizzle-dust in order to return to growing by the time the noon hour was over. And each day it said to itself:

"I must be doing something wrong. Something I do upsets the Wizzles or else I have just not learned to grow. I must work harder."

One day, however, Oranzee—who was tired from all the growing and hungry from missing so many meals—lost control of itself as the Wizzles tracked Wizzledust across its Arpanzee garden. As it saw all its sturdy Arpanzees shrivel up and tuck their heads under the ground, it felt it just could not stand it any more! It stomped its foot, flung its hands away from its round body, opened its mouth, and screeched:

"Stop it! Stop it! I can't stand it! Keep out of my garden! Never come in here again!"

Then it subsided into choking and grunting as it realized what a display it had made for a Quizzle. (Quizzles sometimes did things like that—but not as often as Wizzles said they did—and certainly no one behaved this way in the gardens!)

The Wizzles stood back in amazement. They cast astonished looks at each other. They looked slightly frightened for never had they seen a Wizzle behave in this way (Wizzles never stomped and flung and screeched, they only enlarged in size, turned from yellow to green, and looked quite fierce as their angry voices made the earth tremble). Then they laughed:

"Well, after all it's only a Quizzle. It is true, Quizzles belong at the hearth."

And they continued walking through Oranzee's garden going to their noonday meal dutifully prepared by the hearthbound Quizzles.

Oranzee was so ashamed. "I am wrong again," it said to itself. "Maybe I have no business growing." Oranzee gave a deep sigh and in so doing drew all the blue outside right into itself. It hung its head on its round body, dropped its already rounded shoulders, and went back to sit at the hearth by the pots. But it did not condense, and when the worktime came around again, it did not grow either. It just sat . . . and sat . . . and sat.

Finally, however, Oranzee's round bottom grew tired of just sitting, its hands grew tired of hanging, its shoulders tired of drooping. Without knowing what it was doing, it began stirring the pot. "This is where I belong," it said. "I have no right to grow."

But the longer it stirred the pot, the more it wished it was back in the garden. It looked at the pink Arpanzees condensing in the pot and yearned to see the bright red Arpanzees in the garden. Oranzee imagined all those heads peeking up, stretching to reach the sun. Then it remembered: Its Arpanzees would not be reaching for the sun. Its Arpanzees would be tucking their heads under the Wizzledust! And Orzanee's shoulders dropped again and a tear rolled down its round cheek right into the condensing pot. As more tears poured into the pot, some splashed onto the fire beneath the pot, putting out the fire and ruining the condensing. Then a hard thought, a rectangular thought, prodded at Oranzee's spherical self.

As the rectangular thought grew, Oranzee's legs straightened, its shoulders squared, and its chin stuck out over its round body (which was pretty good for a Quizzle because, as the great intellects of the Wizzle world say, round chins are not for sticking out) and it said to itself:

"I am going to march right back and take care of my Arpanzees! I am going to grow!"

So the rectangular part of Oranzee (which could not be seen from the outside) marched its round body right back to its garden. With every step, it pushed more of the blue right out of itself. Then as the sun set over Wizzledom, Oranzee could be seen clearing the Wizzledust from its garden and whispering kind words to the bewildered Arpanzees who had almost given up hope that they might ever raise their heads again. It was almost as if the words Oranzee spoke were responded to by the Arpanzees; a bond was created between them in which they each promised to help the other grow (and you can imagine what a Wizzle would make of that idea!).

The next morning, Oranzee approached its garden with determination and worked hard until the Panzee Hour planning strategies with which to keep the Wizzles out of its garden. It searched for an idea. It thought of a fence, but this would keep out the Wizzlewater brought by carts at Panzee-Hour-minus-two. No cart could enter through a fence. Oranzee pondered. Perhaps it could bring in Wizzlewater itself. But this had never been done and, even if it could do so, it would be working through the night as well as through the Panzee Hour. "So much for fences," said Oranzee bluely to itself.

"What *shall* I do?" Oranzee said to itself. "There is no place to turn for help." *No* place? *No* place at all? "Well, certainly not Wizzles," Oranzee answered itself (ignoring the fact that some Wizzles might want to help). "And not hearthbound Quizzles either!" it continued. No place? No place at all? The question still continued from somewhere inside Oranzee. Then a wide and round smile on Oranzee's orange face pushed the blue away. "Of course," it said, "there must be other growing Quizzles. I will find them and together we will think of something to do!"

As Oranzee thought this, the Panzee Hour was struck and all the gardening Wizzles marched for the hearth, four of them striding right for Oranzee's garden. Oranzee was angry and sad all at the same time but did not let the blue creep into its determined body. Spurred on by its new plan and its concern for its Arpanzees, it stood up very straight (for a round being) and stood directly in the path of the Wizzles.

"Stop! You are not coming into my garden again!"

It said this in a strong voice that made the earth tremble, just like a Wizzle. The Wizzles stopped, astonished once again. But they retreated and walked w-a-a-a-y around the outside of the garden. As they did so they laughed to each other and snickered at such behavior from a Quizzle. Who did it think it was? A Wizzle?

Oranzees' round body trembled with relief. Yet it was not glad. It did not want to act like a Wizzle! Did it have to change its voice, squeeze in its round body, and cause the earth to tremble in order to grow? Oranzee hoped not. As soon as the sun set that evening and it spoke a few kind words to the Arpanzees now gently tucked under for the night, it set out to find other growing Quizzles.

Oranzee traveled far into the evening, moving from gardenhood to gardenhood and in almost every gardenhood it found at least one growing Quizzle. It asked all the growing Quizzles to gather at its hearth after the next day's work was done. The other Quizzles each looked tired and worn out, but there was something exciting about seeing another growing Quizzle and each in turn said yes.

The next evening, after a tiring day fending off Wizzles and their Wizzledust, Oranzee met with eight other growing Quizzles. Each Quizzle was very nice to the others and each complimented Oranzee on its hearth (hearths, after all, belong to the world of Quizzles). None of the growing Quizzles acted any differently from the other hearthbound Quizzles for all were very Quizzle-like in their roundness and their softness. They were all very cooperative, at least on the surface. This behavior is a lesson all Quizzles learn well and which is very hard to unlearn. Anyway growing Quizzles were brand new at talking to each other about anything but hearths and pots and how it felt to be condensing, and how troublesome it was to take care of big Wizzles and little Wizzles, and all the time winking at each other because they knew Quizzles were really better than Wizzles. So this familiar behavior went on for some time until the Quizzles thought it was almost time to go.

Then Oranzee said, "But we haven't talked about the business of the meeting yet." The Quizzles looked at the sky and said it was getting late and looked at each other and looked at Oranzee. Oranzee said, "I have this problem . . ." and it began to tell about the Wizzles and the Wizzledust. As it began to tell its tale, the atmosphere changed, and became less soft and less round and the round Quizzles smiled less and they stopped saying nice, cooperative Quizzle things. All of the Quizzles listened intently and as Oranzee finished, the other Quizzles chimed in, "But that happens to me too."

Time passed and night set in, as Quizzle after Quizzle told the same story. They told of the work they had done, the carelessness of the Wizzles, the strategies they had planned (the pleading, the hysteria, the building of fences, the working through the Panzee Hour) and they talked, too, about equality that reigned throughout the land. As they talked, they moved closer together and their voices grew stronger (but in a Quizzle way, not in a trembling-of-the-earth Wizzle way) and they began to smile at each other until suddenly they exclaimed in unison, "Why, nothing is wrong with us! We can grow! But something is wrong with the Wizzles! What are we going to do about it?" They planned and they planned far into the night.

The next morning Oranzee worked in its garden, slightly tired, but with a rosy glow on its orange face and a slightly rectangular look in its round eye. It did not even pay attention to the Wizzles' remarks about Quizzles meeting at night—what were they doing anyway, finding new ways to stir the pot? As the bell rang for Panzee Hour, the Wizzles laid down their tools and started for their hearths again heading right toward Oranzee's plot. But as they approached the garden Oranzee was joined by two other growing Quizzles who had come to carry out the plan as decided the night before. The Quizzles stood round and firm right in the middle of Oranzee's garden talking in round, firm voices to each other. As the Wizzles raised their feet to move into Oranzee's garden, each Quizzle looked up in surprise and said, "Excuse me, I think you are stepping in our garden, and moreover you are interfering with the meeting of Quizzles For Gardens. Would you please walk around?" With this statement each Quizzle, looking very round and very firm and not cooperative at all, turned back to the other growing Quizzles and continued its discussion. The Wizzles were nonplussed. They had never seen growing Quizzles together before. Why, there were so many of them (two growing Quizzles might be a little overwhelming, so one can see that three is almost terrifying!). What were they talking about? Very carefully, the Wizzles said, "Oh, excuse us. We didn't know this was your garden," and walked around the edges.

The next day at Panzee Hour, Oranzee was joined again by two other members of the new association Quizzles For Gardens. (This meant, of course, that the others' gardens were empty for the moment, but would soon be occupied by another shift of growing Quizzles.) The Wizzles looked out of the corners of their eyes at these Quizzles and carefully walked around the garden. When they were out of earshot of the Quizzles, they looked at each other:

"What are the Quizzles talking about? Growing??? Quizzles don't grow—not really!" But as they said this, their rectangular faces looked a little less rectangular and their shoulders a little less square.

"Perhaps they were talking about big Wizzles and little

Wizzles?" They looked with consternation at each other. "They wouldn't say we walked across their gardens on purpose! We hardly knew they were gardens!" They shook their heads at each other and made for the hearths. They did not understand this new turn of events and were very puzzled and slightly upset by the whole thing (though they would not admit that even to themselves). In the future they were very careful to leave the Quizzles' gardens alone. Quizzles who did not behave like Quizzles! And more than one of them!! And growing! This was beyond the comprehension of any truly rectangular Wizzle.

However, just as the Wizzles left Oranzee's garden alone, so the Wizzles in every gardenhood of the land began to walk around the gardens of other growing Quizzles since at every Quizzle-garden groups of growing Quizzles firmly and politely told them *not* to track Wizzledust across the gardens. The Wizzles did not understand this at all—it appeared as if the Quizzles were really *serious* about growing. These Quizzles also were acting in completely unpredictable ways—who ever heard of a Quizzle who did not smile and nod or plead and screech, or turn bright orange when a Wizzle approached? The Wizzles left the growing Quizzles completely alone. But leaving the Quizzles alone was not particularly new since they had never known what to do with the growing Quizzles anyway. They were happier in some ways to leave them alone than to continue to tweak their ears, pat their backs, and smirk at them.

But after a while the Wizzles came to notice that the Quizzles were also leaving *them* strictly alone! (Throughout the history of Wizzledom no Quizzle had ever ignored a Wizzle—at least not for long and certainly not if it was a *normal* Quizzle.) Moreover, the Quizzles appeared to be having a good time together and their Arpanzee gardens were bright and red and some were rather splendid. It appeared that the Quizzles knew something Wizzles did not know about raising Arpanzees. Some of the Wizzles (in particular, those who had always suspected they were not hard and rectangular all the way through, though they had never acknowledged this aloud) thought that it might be a good idea to join the Quizzles. Maybe Quizzles are good for other things besides tweaking and patting and condensing, they thought. (As has been pointed out before, some Wizzles had always suspected this anyway.) But the last thought was quickly jerked back under the rectangular Wizzle-cover and did not emerge again for quite a while.

After all they were Wizzles, not Quizzles, and many were very frightened by the thought that if they were not Wizzles all the way through they might be Quizwizzles or Wizquizzles! They shuddered at the thought, straightened their rectangular bodies and puffed themselves up, causing the earth to tremble. Thus did they reassure themselves about the natural order of things.

Meanwhile the Quizzles continued to meet. Each Quizzle looked forward to the meetings. Each felt excited by the discussions and left the meetings knowing that though it was round it was firm, and though it was orange, it was still a good grower of red Arpanzees. As the meetings continued, each growing Quizzle came to know deep inside that it was not wrong for Quizzles to grow but that it was doing exactly the right thing for itself! In addition, all the Quizzles took pride in the fact that they were learning to live in the gardens of Wizzles and that they did not have to be like Wizzles— nor like hearthbound Quizzles either—and that it was really all right, in fact, very exciting, to grow. The excitement of their new discoveries bound them together for quite some time. The Wizzles, still slightly curious, very puzzled, and just a bit envious, sometimes wished that they could join the Quizzles. None ever said so, however, and in their hard rectangular way they continued to ignore the Quizzles and to wonder, occasionally, about the natural order of things.

After a period of time in the land of Wizzledom, the work of growing Quizzles came to be an accepted but puzzling part of the nature of things. No one except the growing Quizzles themselves felt that growing Quizzles were really doing what they were *supposed* to be doing. But no one said so, and a slightly uneasy peace came to rest upon the land and the purplish-blue atmosphere lost some of its bluish tinge.

Yet a new problem was developing in the midst of the Quizzles who grew and who met with each other every week or so. Quizzles, of course, as mentioned previously, thought of themselves as round, soft, and cooperative. They believed that they were sharing beings who always held the welfare of other beings in mind. They had all learned this in their sling as they lay, as very small Wizzles, by the pots watching the older Quizzles share with each other. Yet somewhere along the way, they had also noticed that when another Quizzle was not looking, sometimes one Quizzle would drip a little Quizzlefloss in another Quizzle's pot, and on that day the other Quizzle would serve up less savory orange Arpanzees instead of the usual pink ones. Sometimes, too, one Quizzle would bump or tip another's pot so that part of the Panzee Hour meal wound up on the hearth instead of in the stomachs of the Wizzles and made a dreadful mess for the Quizzle whose pot was bumped to clean up. Yet, the Quizzles never acknowledged such unQuizzle-like behavior. They smiled roundly at each other as they affirmed how cooperative they were towards each other, being of course only spherical beings.

So it came to pass that the growing Quizzles had come to think of themselves as cooperative sharing beings with round smiles who would never think of putting Quizzlefloss in another's pot nor tracking Quizzlefloss on another's garden nor allowing a Wizzle to bring its dust across a Quizzle garden. Yet now that the earlier crisis of the growing Quizzles had passed, *sometimes they did*. Soon these Quizzles, for they talked often among each other, came to say hard, rectangular, and very sharp things to each other especially when one growing Quizzle had a better garden than another, or when one Quizzle talked longer at the meetings, or when one Quizzle was asked for advice more than another. In fact, the Quizzles found that part of each one was not round, soft, and cooperative but hard, sharp, and quite pointed and willing to do damage to another.

Now, among Quizzles as a whole this was not necessarily a new phenomenon. Quizzles had always done each other in—that is, once in a while when nobody was looking, even as they smiled their round smiles and said their sharing words. This was definitely a Quizzle-phenomenon, not belonging to the Wizzles, who treated each other in hard and rectangular ways but not sharp and pointed ones. Moreover, when a Wizzle was very hard and rectangular with another Wizzle that Wizzle and all the other Wizzles knew about it and commented upon it and nobody said any nonsense about being round and cooperative and sharing. Sometimes the Wizzles treated each other kindly and sometimes they did not, but they never made any bones about it. Sometimes the Quizzles treated each other kindly and sometimes they did not, and yet they had always, through all history, pretended that this was not so.

This attitude about Quizzleness permeated the group led by Oranzee and its friends and soon they began treating each other in sharp and pointed ways. *Once* they refused to join a Quizzle threatened by Wizzledust. Once again Wizzles tracked Wizzledust across the garden of a Quizzle and nobody stood in their way and calmly commented about the business of growing Arpanzees. Oranzee, in particular, was very concerned about this recent turn of events. "Why, we will be right back where we started!" it thought to itself and it hurriedly called a very important meeting of the Quizzles for the next Panzee Hour.

The next day at the Panzee Hour, the growing Quizzles gathered at Oranzee's hearth and complimented it about its hearth and dripped a little Quizzlefloss into its pot, and bumped its pot just a little, so a few pink Arpanzees fell onto the stones beneath, and they smiled at each other as nice cooperative Quizzles do. Oranzee watched this behavior and once again felt the skies darken and the blue threaten to invade its being, but soon it rounded out its chest and opened its round mouth, and said in a round firm Quizzle-voice: "Stop! Don't you see what a terrible thing is happening to us?" The other Quizzles looked astonished and puzzled and said no they did not see anything at all. Weren't they all very happy together and weren't they all grateful to Oranzee and the other growing Quizzles for helping them to defend their gardens? Everything seemed to be just fine. They smiled roundly at each other.

Oranzee scarcely knew what to do since it also wanted to be round and soft and cooperative and join with the other Quizzles in their familiar talk of little Wizzles and big Wizzles and condensing pots—for the Quizzles, now that the initial danger of Wizzledust was past, had returned to their familiar ways learned in their slings at the older Quizzles' condensing pots. But Oranzee saw that if it did this all would be lost and eventually it and the other growing Quizzles would return to the hearths and give up their right to grow.

So Oranzee said, "Listen! I want to say something." And here it choked and stammered a little for it was about to say a very unQuizzle-like thing. "I am angry," it said. "I am angry that you put Quizzlefloss in my pot and bumped my condensing Arpanzees and I am angry that you are pretending everything is quite all right when it is not!"

The other Quizzles' mouths fell open and they bumped

Oranzee's pot again, for they were very upset and very un-comfortable and slowly turning from orange to green as their round chests heaved up and down. Nobody who had any notion of Quizzleness at all ever said they were angry in that straightforward way. Rather Quizzles (who were main-taining their Quizzleness) always screeched and flung and stomped when they were angry and were very sorry after-wards, or else they dropped Quizzlefloss and bumped pots in sharp, pointed ways while still believing that they were soft and round. So now, without knowing what to do, the other Quizzles were angry too and looked with suspicion at Oranzee.

"Now," Oranzee said, "that was a very hard thing for me to do. I would like to talk about it some more. What are you feeling? Are you angry?"

"Oh, no," said the other Quizzles, looking sharp and pointed but smiling roundly, "We are not. We are not. We are very happy to have you as a friend and colleague," and they bumped its pot again.

But another Quizzle, sitting back, had some notion what Oranzee was talking about. It was hard, too, for this Quizzle to say what it was thinking, but it did. It said, "Wait, all of you. It is true that I am angry. And I feel upset. And I would like to bump your pot, Oranzee, for upsetting the order or Quizzleness. But," this very wise Quizzle went on, "I think that I am not so much angry as I am scared. I do not know how not to be round and smiling and I do not know what to do when I feel sharp and pointed except to bump another's pot and drop Quizzlefloss. Oranzee, I am feeling angry but I think that is because I am scared to change the way I have always been."

Then all the Quizzles talked. They said, timidly at first, and then more boldly, that they were angry and scared too but they did not want to lose the fruits (or Arpanzees) of their labors and did not want to give up the right to grow.

All these changes in the ways of the world had indeed become very frightening and so they did not know what to do but to bump each other's pots. Oranzee nodded and said it felt the same way but if they were to continue to grow they would have to find a way to be straightforward about the nonQuizzlelike parts of themselves.

Over the next weeks, the growing Quizzles met and talked about their anger, at each other and at the Wizzles. They talked about their hurt, at the actions of each other and those of the Wizzles. Occasionally one even mentioned how it liked to be noticed for its successes (an astonishing statement, since only Wizzles share their successes; Quizzles talk always about their failures which reminds everyone that they only have others in mind and are not boastful and bragging like the Wizzles) and sometimes how it felt competitive with other Quizzles, and even the Wizzles.

As the weeks went by the Quizzles realized that they were not wholly spherical and soft; also inside was the hard and rectangular part of themselves which had first prodded Oranzee to begin its association with other Quizzles. As they came to recognize the hard and rectangular part, it blended in with the round and spherical part; there was hardly ever a need to be sharp and pointed all the time maintaining that they were round and cooperative. And so these Quizzles came to set an example to each other and even to the hearthbound Quizzles about being whole beings rather than part beings. Occasionally they had trouble being hard and competitive but found that when they said they were, the hardness did not have to find its way out in a pointy way, but blended with the softness into a nice firm combination, and the rectangular part of themselves came to be a regular part of the spherical Quizzles.

Meanwhile back at the gardens, the Wizzles were noticing the progress of the Quizzles though they did not realize fully what it was about. They knew however that their attempts to walk across Quizzle gardens were stopped again. They knew that sometimes they saw the Quizzles arguing (astonishing enough in itself) and then going about their work together when the argument was over as if they did not even intend to sprinkle Quizzlefloss in each others' pots, and they saw the Quizzles' gardens bloom once more.

As they watched the Quizzles, those Wizzles who had first noticed the round, spherical part of their insides (who were often the same Wizzles who had once offered to help the Quizzles) wanted very much to talk to the Quizzles and see why their Arpanzees grew so well but they did not know how. Maybe the Quizzles would again say "No!" The Wizzles were scared of that, but pretended instead that they really did not care about the Quizzles. But one Wizzle (for there are truly wise Wizzles just as there are wise Quizzles) said to itself, "Yes, I am scared—but I'm not going to let that stop me!" and it headed toward Oranzee's garden.

As it approached Oranzee and the other Quizzles drew up in its path, the Wizzle said, "Wait, please. I am very interested in what you are doing. I do not want to track Wizzledust all over the place. I want to join you if I may." The Quizzles looked astonished and they looked at each other. They looked at this Wizzle and, as they did, they saw that it was straight and rectangular and in its own way rather attractive. Each Quizzle felt something sharp and pointy grow within. Quickly each said, "We must talk this over. Would you please come back tomorrow?"

The Quizzles turned to each other and looked hard at each other and felt all the pointy things they once again felt like saying to the other Quizzles, because a *Wizzle*, and an attractive one at that, had come into their garden. They had a hard time with the pointy thoughts which prodded at their spherical outsides saying things like, "Well, if you smile roundly and sweetly and drop enough Quizzlefloss in the way of other Quizzles, maybe the Wizzle will like *you* best!"

Each Quizzle felt the same way for they had all learned long ago in their slings that each Quizzle was to try its very best to get an attractive Wizzle to stand at its side—and, in such moments, being round to other Quizzles (all the way through, not just on the outside) did not count—not one bit.

But this time the desire for the attractive Wizzle and the hard pointy side of the Quizzles came up against something entirely new in the history of Quizzles—it came up against the new and growing part of the Quizzles which had learned to talk and to share and to respect other Quizzles. They realized that once again there were more things under the sun than they had learned of in their slings, and slowly each growing Quizzle started to chuckle and then to laugh and each Quizzle looked at every other Quizzle and soon they reached out and hugged the other Quizzles and they all laughed together.

Then they talked. It was exciting that a Wizzle wanted to join them since that would only make the growing of Arpanzees easier and would enlarge their circle of beings who did not ignore them and who shared the knowledge and the chit-chat that accompanied the growing of Arpanzees. They knew too that if ever growing Quizzles were to be accepted (not just tolerated, but accepted) in all the land, they would have to stop being just growing Quizzles but become growing beings. So the next day when the Wizzle returned, a little hesitantly and not so rectangularly as a Wizzle usually is, the growing Quizzles welcomed it into their association and soon it too learned to have fun growing Arpanzees, to talk to its Arpanzees as the Quizzles did (which turned out really splendid red gardens), and to argue and to discuss and often to smile. The association of Quizzles For Gardens, now called Wizzles For Gardens had grown by one—and very happily too.

As the Wizzles watched the other Wizzle and saw that nothing terrible happened and that it did not turn into a

Quizwizzle or a Wizquizzle and that its garden did not shrivel up but bloomed beautifully, one by one other Wizzles came and joined the associations of Wizzles For Gardens. As they did so, they came to recognize the roundness in themselves just as the Quizzles had recognized their rectangular parts, and soon the roundness and rectangularity of each being was recognized far and wide.

This new view of orange and yellow beings soon spread to the hearths where, at first, it greatly upset the hearthbound Quizzles. But soon some hearthbound Quizzles decided to risk an experiment and found that they too were somewhat rectangular inside and that they could argue and discuss and *Grow* and did not need to drop Quizzlefloss in each others' pots or even track Quizzlefloss on each others' new gardens. Soon all the Quizzles and all the Wizzles were *Growing* whether they worked in the gardens or at the hearths and some Wizzles and some Quizzles each did some of both. All the little Wizzles grew up, well cared for by the growing Wizzles and Quizzles, believing that they too could grow whether in the gardens or by the pots, whichever was best for them.

Now this transformation took a very long time and did not happen overnight. But after many Panzee-years the sky over Wizzledom (which was now called Qwizzledom) was once again purplish-pink and all the blue had gone from the land. Contrary to all the popular rumors, which nobody had really believed anyway (or so they said), the natural order of things was changed throughout the land and not even one very red and beautiful Arpanzee went up in a giant fizzle!

And so the Qwizzles of the land, formerly called Wizzles and Quizzles, worked and played more happily together and were both round and soft. Though it was apparent that some Qwizzles were still yellow and rectangular whereas others were orange and spherical, everybody knew that you could not tell a pot, nor an Arpanzee either, by its outside but only by its inside. The insides of all the Wizzles were each very different. But they were also very alike in that each Wizzle was both round and rectangular in the way that it best suited each individual Wizzle. And it came to be that, at least for a period of time (for new conflicts, but resolvable ones, are always brewing where there are growing Wizzles about), everybody lived happily ever after and *Everybody had the right to grow*.

EPILOGUE

Some of you may think that this is a fairy-tale and that such harmony and integration can only exist in lands which have purplish-pink skies, and indeed that may be so. For no one outside of Qwizzledom knows yet, in all the history of all beings, whether or not such a thing can come to pass. But if other wise beings can look deep inside to recognize the parts that do not show on the outside and let these parts be part of the whole—recognizing that we are all scared to change, but that is what living is about—we can all grow just in the way that orange beings and yellow beings have grown—with just a little help from each other.

INDEX